Liquid Legacy

A timeless tribute to the founders of
The United States Bartenders' Guild

Livio Lauro

Copyright © 2023 United States Bartenders' Guild, Inc.
All rights reserved.

This book or any portion thereof may not be copied or reproduced without the express written permission of the United States Bartenders' Guild, Inc.

United States Bartenders' Guild® and Liquid Legacy® are registered trademarks of United States Bartenders' Guild, Inc.

Library of Congress Control Number: 2023913488
ISBN: 979-8-218-24882-6

First published in 2023 by:
United States Bartenders' Guild, Inc.
2654 W. Horizon Ridge Parkway
Ste B5, PMB 252
Henderson, NV 89052
www.usbg.org

Printed in China

Every effort has been made to identify and contact the copyright holders of images in this book. Any errors or omissions to the credits are unintentional and the publisher would be grateful if notified of any corrections that should be incorporated into future edits or reprints of this book; such notifications may be directed to the United States Bartenders' Guild.

To all the bartenders from around the world who fight for what they believe in, even when it is invisible to others.

CONTENTS

VI	Foreword by Jose Ancona
VIII	Preface
001	Prologue
004	Chapter One: The Founding of the UKBG
010	Chapter Two: Post Prohibition Era
016	Chapter Three: Dawn of the Guild
028	Chapter Four: The California Bartenders' Guild
044	Chapter Five: The USBG and its First Golden Era
052	Chapter Six: The WTF Era
074	Epilogue
077	Recipes From Past Guild Members
130	Bibliography
131	Acknowledgements
132	Index

Jose F. Ancona (1933 - 2020)

FOREWORD

By Jose Ancona

I met Livio Lauro in 1999 when he was tending bar in San Pedro, California. It was a ritual to welcome new members by visiting them at their bar. Livio had joined the USBG years prior but was fresh "off the boat" from Italy, so I thought it would be a great idea to introduce myself.

I was quickly struck by his drive and charisma, so I took him under my wing to help him adapt to his new life and flourish in his career. That's what fellow Guild members do; we help our peers.

In July 2001, I accompanied Livio to Malaga, Spain, where he competed in the World Finals of the *Bacardi-Martini Grand Prix*, which was known as the most difficult cocktail competition of the time, featuring 60 of the world's top bartenders from 20 countries. The US had never taken a medal in this competition since its inception in 1966. That year, Livio brought home America's first medal in the "Paissa" category (bartenders 35 years old or younger). He was in good company, as Dale DeGroff and Tony Abou-Ganim were also victorious in different categories.

In 2005, Livio became the national president of the USBG at a very challenging time in our history. The Guild needed new leadership and young blood. Livio's term represented the biggest comeback in the Guild's history; by 2009 the Guild had reached its highest number of chapters, members, and revenue. The enthusiasm in his term culminated with the launching of the USBG's certification program.

I have always known Livio as a great bartender and a fantastic leader for our Guild. But I recently discovered his ability to research our industry and write books.

The book you are holding is a work of art and depicts some of our past members' lives and their epic cocktails. While the rich history of our Guild cannot be traced back in its entirety, this collection is an amazing celebration of what was accomplished in the first 50 years. If you are a bartender, you need to read this book.

Jose F. Ancona
Co-Founder, Past President, and Lifetime Member of the United States Bartenders' Guild
Past Vice-President for North America of the International Bartender's Association
Bartender for 56 years – Guild member since 1965

PREFACE

The year 2023 marks 75 years since America's premier bartenders guild was founded, and this book is a tribute to the first 50 years of that legacy.

One of the stories that I have always been fascinated with comes from the great Luca Picchi. In his book *Negroni Cocktail: An Italian Legend*, Luca explains that he gained his inspiration to research the history of the Negroni cocktail when, on a random day, he came across an old picture of a sign of the *Café Casoni* in Florence. It was from there that his tireless research of this iconic cocktail and the lives of those involved in its creation started. The picture simply depicts a shielded sign hanging outdoors, and it sparked a fire in him to uncover the true history of this cocktail and share it with the world.

Life is full of surprises and one day in 2015, as I was window shopping on *eBay*, I came across a picture of six bartenders boarding a United Airlines plane with an American shield patch on their jacket pockets. It gave me a strange feeling of excitement and my attention had been piqued.

I could not stop digging for more information. That information turned out to be the most intriguing scavenger hunt I have ever been involved in, a story of bartenders of the past, their contributions to the American cocktail, and a fascinating tie to a profession I love.

Most of the events that I reveal in this book were fueled by cocktails as the social lubricant, therefore nobody was too worried about taking notes. As a result, relying on the testimonies would only get me so far. As I picked the brains of some of the key characters of this story, their recollections of what happened at any given event were so convincingly different that it was nearly impossible to pick who to believe.

This does not surprise me. When I was interviewed for a video documentary to celebrate the 15-year anniversary of the founding of the Las Vegas Chapter of the USBG, I told the story as I remembered it. However, it turned out that they had also interviewed a few other co-founders, and not one of our stories matched. The storytellers found it hilarious, but those who wanted to know how it all really happened did not.

To assemble this timeline, I have relied heavily on old articles, program books, and meeting minutes that helped connect the dots of the story.

This story of the USBG has been greatly enhanced by the six bartenders who have contributed to the book. Their riffed-on versions of six historical cocktails that have special ties to the Guild have greatly enriched my work. Those six folks are Bridget Albert, Charles Joly, Jen Ackrill, Julio Cabrera, Tiffanie Barriere, and Martin Cate. I truly hope you enjoy the events, rituals, and cocktails from this book as much as I have enjoyed compiling them.

Livio Lauro

1914 World War I / 1939 World War II

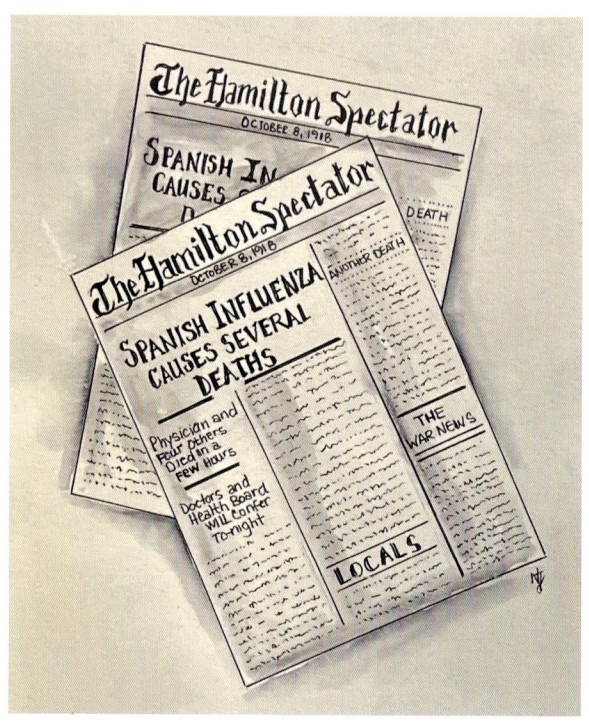

1918 - 1919 The Spanish Flu

PROLOGUE

A whirlwind of craziness

The first decade of the 20th century was like the calm before the storm. Productivity was increasing and the global economy was great and better than it had ever been before.[1] There was still much to improve socially and politically, but many things seemed to be headed in the right direction. The Second Industrial Revolution started in 1908 when Henry Ford began production on the Model T Ford using the assembly line to build the first affordable automobile.

The hospitality industry was also up-ticking locally and globally. New taverns and places to drink were continuing to pop up, and as those establishments increased, so did the number of people who were employed in them.[2]

These employees often felt the need to meet and discuss professional matters. These discussions developed into regular meetings and groups started to form. As early as 1909, five enthusiastic bartenders (three German and two American) formed the *International Barkeepers Union* (IBU) in Cologne, Germany.

In 1914, progress had to make a fast stop, and the world had to deal with the First World War. It lasted four years and took the lives of 20 million people: this kickstarted a global downturn.

Between 1918 and 1919, the Spanish Flu infected an estimated 500 million people, killing nearly 10% of them with an estimated 675,000 occurring in the United States.[3] This pandemic further altered consumer behavior, created uncertainty, and made it particularly difficult to maintain food inventories. Fresh fruit, vegetables, meat, and bread were hard to find.

Rebounding back to world peace, normal lives, and consumer confidence after these two tragic events was not going to be easy, especially with a Second World War around the corner. In fact, further disruption came in 1939, with World War II. It was the deadliest military conflict in history, lasted six years, and took the lives of roughly 80 million people. This was yet another burden on food supplies, amongst many other socio-economic challenges.[4]

At times like this a good cocktail is the most important of the least important things. The tragic events which devastated the hospitality industry and the culinary art of that era – and just about every other industry and family which were burdened by this whirlwind of craziness – is inconceivable. Can you imagine just how hard it would have been to enjoy life in the company of family, friends, good food, and drinks during these times?

As if things weren't bad enough, America also had two more hospitality-killing events to add. The 1930s brought the south-central United States six years of drought-affected dust storms. The aftermath was known as "The Dust Bowl," because the dust drifted like snow, covering farm buildings and houses. Nineteen states, in the heartland of the United States, were affected.

---

1. J. Bradford DeLong, 2000, Cambridge, MA, The Shape of Twentieth Century Economic History, Working Paper 7569 National Bureau of Economic Research, http://www.nber.org/papers/w7569
2. John G. Van Hagen, The Bols Book of Cocktails (Nieuw-Vennep, NL: Bols Royal Distilleries, 1992), pp 26-27
3. https://my.clevelandclinic.org/health/diseases/21777-spanish-flu Last accessed on 29 April 2023.
4. https://w.wiki/6eC9. Last accessed on 4/29/23

The drought's most severe period was between 1934 and 1935, and in those two years alone, an estimated 1.2 billion tons of soil were lost across 100 million acres of the Great Plains.[5] Across the entire country, people were out of work, production was down, and commodities were scarce. Because there were no large-scale programs that could distribute unused food, many crops went to waste, despite widespread poverty and hunger.

People simply couldn't catch a break at this time, and just in case they were looking for an alcoholic drink to soften the blow, the 66th Congress of the United States designed and voted in "the noble experiment" of American Prohibition. This self-inflicted wound lasted from Jan 17, 1920, to Dec 5, 1933, and strictly prohibited the production, importation, transportation, and sale of alcoholic beverages. Now, people couldn't drink booze, and Prohibition brought a rise in organized crime, an increase in smuggling, and a decline in tax revenue.[6]

Now that I have painted a picture to recap these 31 years of craziness, who can we point the finger at if there was no fresh food in people's kitchens in the 1950s? After all, most households only recently had access to processed foods like Spam, frozen dinners, and canned foods. The canned foods were, at first, a very convenient commodity to send to the troops overseas and after the wars were over, they became a convenient staple of America's diet.[7]

This was the gloom of the first half of the twentieth century. The recent COVID-19 pandemic has given us a small window into how life-changing events like these create emotional exhaustion. In just two years, so many career plans got tangled, and ambitions diminished.

American Prohibition ironically also had a positive effect on the global drinking scene. It forced the skilled bartenders of the United States to flee the country and practice their craft overseas. Particularly blessed with the services and talents of these craftsmen were the cities of Paris, Havana, and London, amongst others. Skilled bartenders left the country, but the need for their craft increased. American Prohibition popularized cocktails because the alcohol available at the time was poorly made. It was either homemade or purchased on the black market; in either case it was of inferior quality. This required it to be mixed to make the drinks taste good.

Thirsty Americans started ordering more cocktails in their speakeasies than they did at bars prior to the ban. Additionally, the birth of the speakeasy allowed for men and women alike to be part of the same party—this was something rarely seen before, as women were not allowed in bars.

Outside of the US, there were no restrictions on drinking alcohol. Mixed drinks and cocktails were in fashion in the larger cities of Europe, as well as Cairo, Singapore, Johannesburg, Sydney, and Havana.[8] In cities like these, the time had come to start recreating bartending-related groups and clubs to kickstart the progress that had been sought out towards the end of the previous century.

In 1924, the Bartenders Club of the Republic of Cuba was officially founded in Havana; then came Austria in 1926, and Switzerland in 1927. In 1933, the first steps were taken to form a Guild in Great Britain, and the following year, the United Kingdom Bartenders' Guild (UKBG) was founded.[9]

---

5. https://www.britannica.com/place/Dust-Bowl Last accessed on 26 Dec 2022.
6. https://education.blogs.archives.gov/2016/01/28/prohibition-and-consequences/ Last accessed on 26 Dec 2022.
7. https://www.lovefood.com/gallerylist/92722/canned-foods-america-grew-up-on Last accessed on 26 Dec 2022.
8. https://www.foodandwine.com/news/prohibition-legacy-100th-anniversary Last accessed on 26 Dec 2022
9. John G. Van Hagen, The Bols Book of Cocktails (Nieuw-Vennep, NL: Bols Royal Distilleries, 1992), pp 26-27

1930s The Dust Bowl

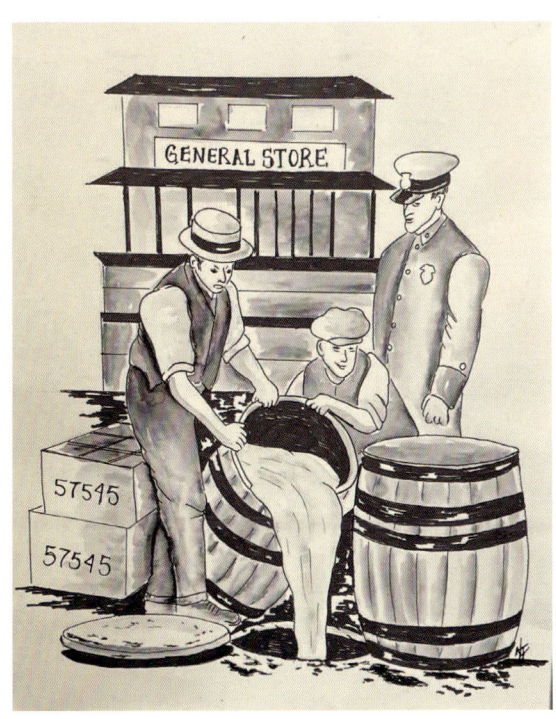
Prohibition officers dumping alcohol

CHAPTER ONE

THE FOUNDING OF THE UKBG (1933–1934)

From top, left to right:
UKBG Magazine Cover 1953;
The Savoy Cocktail Book by Harry Craddock, Constable and Co, 1930;
Copy of UKBG Membership Certificate presented to new members;
Café Royal Cocktail Book by William J. Tarling Publications from Pall Mall Ltd, 1937;

THE UNITED KINGDOM BARTENDERS GUILD

UKBG

THIS IS TO CERTIFY THAT

GERALD FITZPATRICK

is an APPRENTICE MEMBER
of the
UNITED KINGDOM BARTENDERS GUILD

given under the SEAL of the GUILD
this day of APRIL 10th 1948.

President.

Vice President

Secretary

THIS CERTIFICATE IS ISSUED SUBJECT TO THE RULES AND CAN BE CANCELLED BY ORDER OF THE COUNCIL

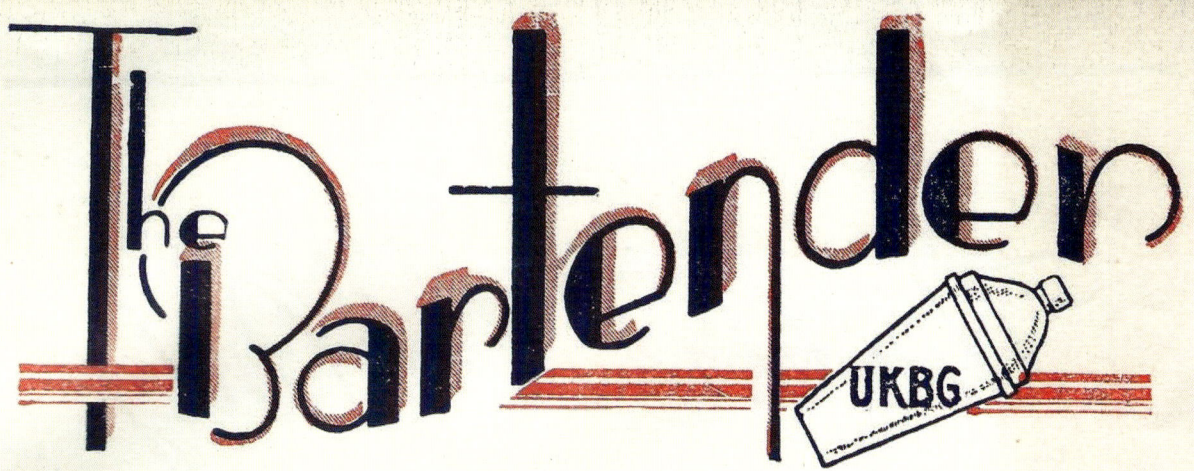

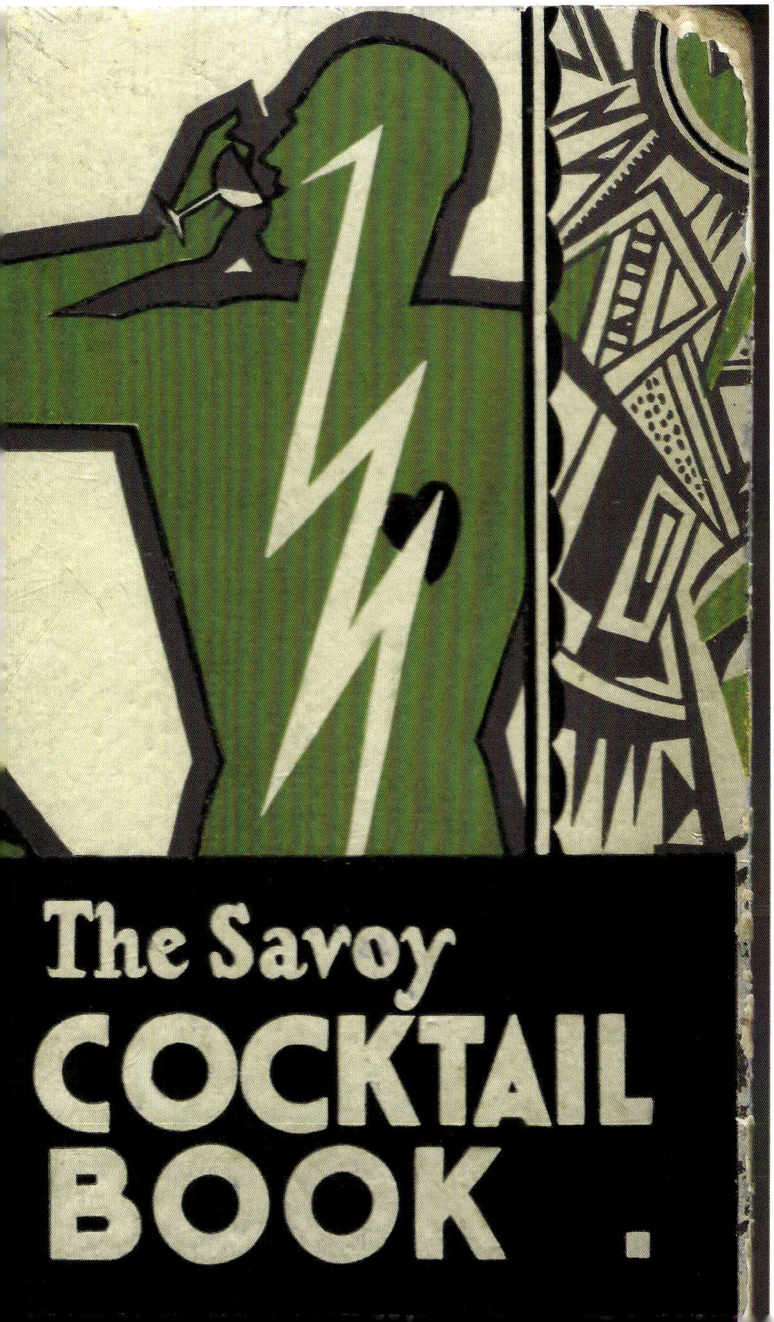

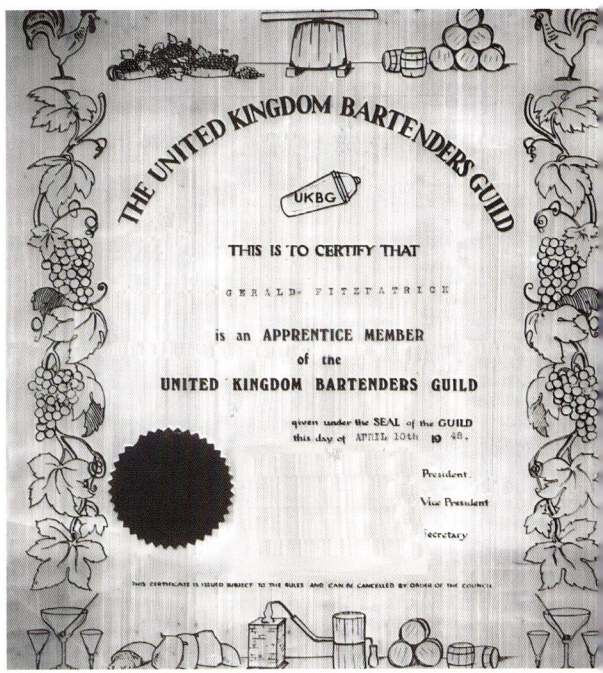

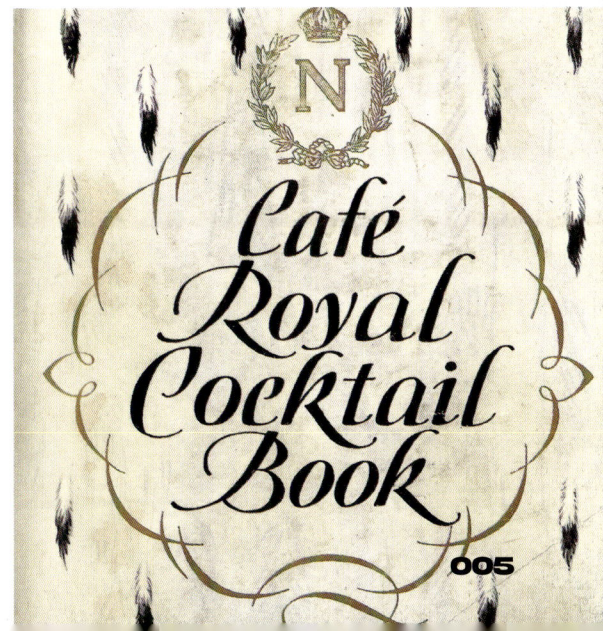

A Legacy Logo of the U.K.B.G.

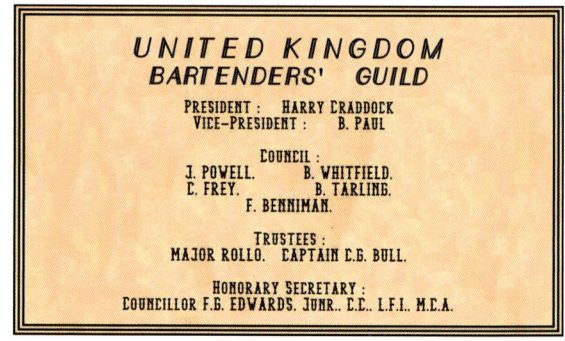

A reproduction of the first UKBG Board as printed on the first issue of *The Bartender* in August 1934

England was familiar with the term "cocktail" dating back to 1798. It was listed in *The Morning Post and Gazette*, an old London-based newspaper that no longer exists. As authors Anistatia Miller and Jared Brown explain in their book, *The Deans of Drinks*, there is more than a good chance that Jerry Thomas, the father of modern bartending, lived in London before moving back to America and writing his groundbreaking 1862 Bartender's Guide, the first cocktail book ever written in America.[10]

During the time that America was fighting Prohibition, the Great Depression, and all the other craft-killing events in the 1920s and early 1930s America, British bartenders, inspired by "iced American drinks," picked up the craft and honored it to the gills. The cocktail scene in London was at the very top of European drinking and beyond.

In October of 1933, the Wine, Spirit, and Catering Trades Exhibition perked up the desire to create something special for the bartending community. The exhibition was held at the Dorland Hall on Lower Regent Street in London—a prestigious venue at the time, and the home for organizing some of London's most important exhibitions. That year, the three-day event included a cocktail competition as one of its featured events, and this competition peaked a lot of interest amongst bartenders and enthusiasts who attended it. At this competition, a line-up of four international cocktail experts were called upon to judge it: William "Bill" Tarling, Mr. Bernard Paul, Mr. F. Edwards, and Mr. B. Whitfield.

In 1933, the United Kingdom Bartenders' Guild (UKBG) was born. It officially chartered in August of 1934, with the iconic bartender Harry Craddock at the helm as the founding President. Renowned bartenders Paul Bernard and Bill Tarling were elected founding Vice President and Council Member respectively.[11] These folks were highly competent and respected in the industry. Basically, they were the dream team of cocktail and bartending knowledge.

Bill Tarling would stay involved in the Guild for the rest of his life. He was also one of the 21 bartenders, that in February 1951, cofounded the International Bartenders' Association (IBA). This global bartenders' association is now present in 64 countries with over 50,000 members.

It would be hard, even to this day, to find more competent people to lay the foundation for a bartenders' guild. The founding president injected the newly formed Guild with the highest standards of bartending. He was not alone; a group of other passionate bartenders rolled up their sleeves to start up one of the most iconic bartender groups ever.

To disseminate knowledge of classic cocktails, they published the Guild's official *Book of Approved Cocktails* in 1937, a guide that focused primarily on how to properly make drinks.

One of the passionate bartenders, who helped with the founding of the UKBG at a very early stage, was Egidio "Angus" Angerosa. There will be more about him in the upcoming chapters.

---

10. Anistatia Miller and Jared Brown, 2013, The Deans of Drink Gloucestershire, UK, Mixellany Limited), p 127
11. https://issuu.com/ukbg/docs/summer_edition_1 Last accessed on 29 Apr 2023.

Historical UKBG Member and President: Harry Craddock

Harry Craddock was a world-renowned English bartender, and one of the most influential ones of the 20th century. He was often referred to as the "dean of cocktail shakers."[12] Harry was born in 1875 in Stroud, England, and moved to America in 1897, at the age of 22. While in America, he bartended in Cleveland, Chicago, and New York. Harry worked at the New York landmark Hoffman House, Holland House, and Knickerbocker Hotel, among other venues. America was in the heart of its first golden age of cocktails; Harry enjoyed living in America, so he became a US citizen.

Upon the start of American Prohibition, he moved to London, allegedly after mixing the last legal cocktail before Prohibition took effect. Harry's decision to leave the United States was later explained through a letter he wrote, stating he felt he had been "exiled by Prohibition."[13] He went to work at the Savoy Hotel in London, starting in 1920, in the service bar. The head bartender at that time was the famous Ada "Coley" Coleman. Ada was a high-profile bartender who served drinks to all the elites of the time. Her signature cocktail, the *Hanky Panky*, is a beautiful spirit-forward sipper made with gin, sweet vermouth, and Fernet Branca, served up with an orange twist. I was not able to find any direct interactions between Ada and Harry.

Harry Craddock
- First U.K.B.G. President

In late 1925, the Savoy shut down the American Bar for renovations and announced the retirement of Ada Coleman after more than 20 years of making history. She was replaced by Harry Craddock, who took over the bar and served the thirsty American and European *bon vivants*

In 1930, Harry compiled the cherished Savoy Cocktail Book per request of the management of the Savoy Hotel. Craddock made no money off the book while compiling this vital reference for today's bartender. According to the late Gary "Gaz" Regan, who was an iconic bartending and cocktail writer, "Craddock's book is probably the most important cocktail book of the 20th century, simply because it has preserved many old recipes that might have been lost to history had he not set them down for us."[14]

---

12. Anistatia Miller and Jared Brown, 2013, The Deans of Drink Gloucestershire, UK, Mixellany Limited), p 113
13. Kevin Seeber, 2013. "Exiled by Prohibition": Americans Abroad and Outsiders at Home https://kevinseeber.com/Exiled.pdf
14. https://www.diffordsguide.com/encyclopedia/2345/people/harry-craddock

008

COCKTAILS

CORPSE REVIVER (No. 2.)	¼ Wine Glass Lemon Juice. ¼ Wine Glass Kina Lillet. ¼ Wine Glass Cointreau. ¼ Wine Glass Dry Gin. 1 Dash Absinthe. *Shake well and strain into cocktail glass.* Four of these taken in swift succession will unrevive the corpse again.
COTA COCKTAIL.	¼ Hercules. ¼ Cointreau. ½ Dry Gin. *Shake well and strain into cocktail glass.*
COUNTRY CLUB COOLER.	1 Glass French Vermouth. 1 Teaspoonful Grenadine. 2 Lumps of Ice. *Pour into tumbler and fill up with soda water.*

COCKTAILS

½ Vanilla Ice Cream. ½ Gin. *No ice is necessary ; just shake until thoroughly mixed, and add water or white wine if the concoction is too thick.*	**THE WHITE CARGO COCKTAIL.**
2 Dashes Orange Bitters. 2 Teaspoonsful Anisette. 1 Glass Dry Gin. *Stir well and strain into cocktail glass. Squeeze lemon peel on top.*	**WHITE COCKTAIL.**
¼ Lemon Juice. ¼ Cointreau. ½ Dry Gin. *Shake well and strain into cocktail glass.*	**WHITE LADY COCKTAIL.**

The Corpse Reviver #2 and *The White Lady* are two classic cocktails found in *The Savoy Cocktail Book* that are attributed to Harry Craddock

009

CHAPTER TWO

THE POST PROHIBITION ERA (1934-1946)

From Top, Left to Right:
Drinks, How to Make and How to Serve Them, By Bill Edwards, David McKay Company, 1936;
The Official Mixer's Manual, Patrick Gavin Duffy, Alta Publications, Inc. 1940;
Old Mr. Boston Bartender's Guide, Ben-Burk Inc., 1934;
Burke's Complete Cocktail And Tastybite Recipes, Harman Burney Burke, 1934;
Booklet compiled by Angostura-Wupperman Corporation, 1934;
Burkes Complete Cocktail and Drinking Recipes, 1936

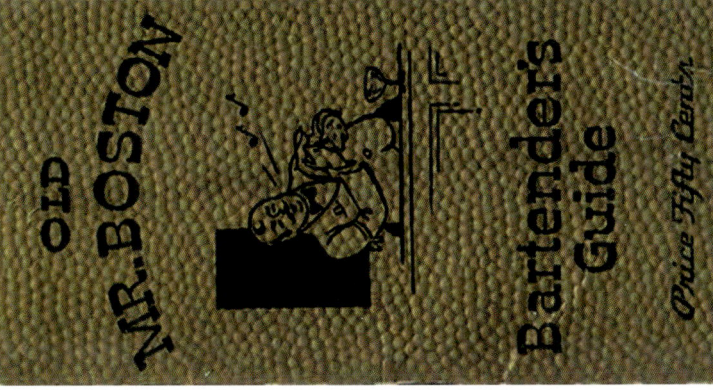
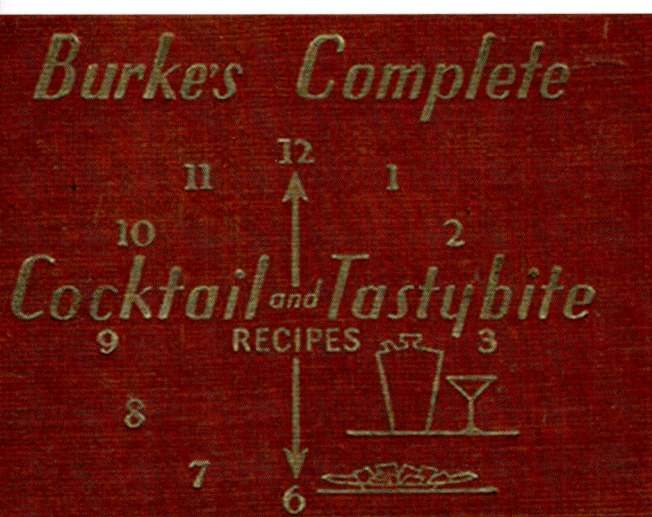

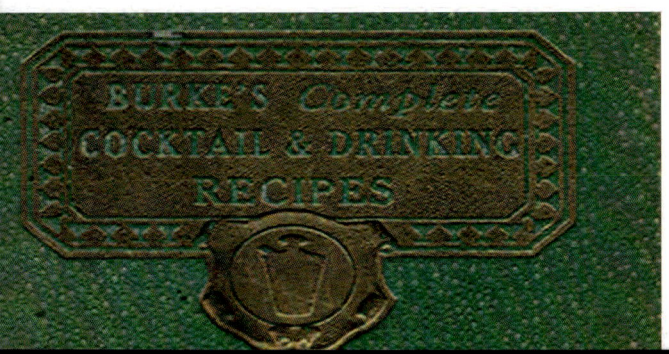

December 5th, 1933 - The End of Prohibition

Prepackaged food available in America in the mid 1900's

On December 5, 1933, the 21st Amendment was ratified; it repealed the 18th Amendment of January 16, 1919. Finally, the piece of legislature that had forced bartenders out of the US was history.

For some of those bartenders, Prohibition was a temporary exile, and repeal meant they could return to America and go back to bartending. For others, however, the consequences of Prohibition lasted much longer. The stigma of criminality that attached itself to the profession remained for decades later.[15] Many bartenders, including Harry Craddock, did not return to America even after Prohibition's repeal. They held the sentiment that they were no longer welcome in the US and could only practice their trade abroad.

Tens of thousands of bartenders likewise came to face a society that viewed their profession as shameful in a way that it had not been before Prohibition. It's easy for me to say this now and was obviously hard to predict at the time; but during all historical moments of gloom in the history of bartending, there are consistently some great things building up and invisible to the naked eye. In 1932, a 26-year-old Filipino emigrant born Valerio Gamet Batugo, who had been moonlighting as a prize fighter; he was an ambitious young man with three big dreams: to fight for a title as a boxer; that his profession as a bartender would become legal; and that he could be a spreader of happiness and hospitality. He would later accomplish all three…

After the repeal of the Volstead Act in 1933, most restaurants and bars went back to squeezing fresh citrus and preparing relatively fresh food. However, the mixology scene was not on par with the past. Only a handful of bartenders were trained to pick up where the professional pre-Prohibition bartenders had left it. To compound the staffing problem, this period also showcased a series of awful new speakeasy recipes designed to mask the taste of bad booze.[16]

Once World War II ended, the packaging industry that was once used to mass produce wartime goods found new life in mass producing food items. This kickstarted the industrialization of food and drink that ramped up in the 1950s and hit a peak by the 1970s. It gave rise to a slew of sour mixes and juices that further tarnished the cocktail scene.[17] During this period, Americans were consuming whatever was handed to them; much of it was packaged food and drinks of terrible quality.

With the exception of the Tiki movement and the great drinks of Don Beach, most drinks in this era sucked. However, the career bartenders who started the bartender's Guild in America were so focused on enhancing the trade, that they did not care what hole the cocktail was in. They were ready to fight the good fight and didn't do it for the glory or the celebrity status, they just had a calling.

---

15. Kevin Seeber, 2013. "Exiled by Prohibition": Americans Abroad and Outsiders at Home https://kevinseeber.com/Exiled.pdf
16. Email interview with Jeff Berry on 2 Jan 2023.
17. https://petroleumservicecompany.com/blog/history-of-canned-food-and-how-it-changed-the-industry/ - Last accessed on 23 Apr 2023.

Historical Member
Egidio "Angus" Angerosa

Soon after cofounding the United Kingdom Bartenders' Guild (UKBG), Egidio Angerosa moved from England to Southern California. Angerosa's first job in the United States was as the head bartender at Stern's Famous BBQ in Culver City, California. A native of Naples, Italy, he went by the name "Angus," and he had a genuine interest in helping others, a reputation he had built while playing a major role in the UKBG. Thanks to this desire of belonging and engaging with people, Angus spearheaded the creation of the California chapter of the UKBG in early 1948.

Angus remained very active in the California chapter of the UKBG, which would later become the United States Bartenders Guild (USBG). He would take on many roles including president and council member and was a stickler of a cocktail judge in the competitions. He would be later be honored with a lifetime membership for his instrumental role as a bartender and a Guild founder. In 1968, he went to work at Hody's Restaurant on La Brea Avenue and Rodeo Road in Los Angeles.

Prior to moving to the US, he developed the *Spider's Web* cocktail (P. 123), published in the *Café Royale Cocktail Book* (1937). During that period, Angus also created the *Banana Bliss* cocktail (P. 081), which soon became popular in the UK and overseas. He also created *Betty Dighton's Mint* cocktail (P. 082) and the *Leg Before Wicket* cocktail (P. 103) that are also published in the *Café Royale Cocktail Book*. These drinks have been included in the recipe section of this book.

Egidio "Angus" Angerosa

SPIDER'S WEB Invented by E. Angerosa	3 dashes Orange Bitters. 1/8 Lemon Juice, fresh. 1/8 Orange Juice, fresh. 1/2 Johnnie Walker Red Label Whisky. 1/4 Golden Apricot Liqueur. Shake.
BETTY DIGHTON'S MINT Invented by E. Angerosa	1/4 Orange Juice, fresh. 5/8 Gordon's Lemon Gin. 1/8 Campari Bitters. 1 Mint Leaf. Shake.
BANANA BLISS Invented by E. Angerosa	1/2 Banana Liqueur, Bols. 1/2 Courvoisier Brandy XXX Shake.
LEG BEFORE WICKET Invented by E. Angerosa	1/12 Campari. 1/12 Lime Juice. 1/6 Dubonnet. 2/3 Gin, Gordon's Dry Special. Mix and strain into cocktail glass. Squeeze Lemon Peel on top.

Four vintage cocktails by Angus printed in the 1937 *Café Royal Cocktail Book*

CHAPTER THREE

THE DAWN OF THE GUILD – THE UK LENDS A HAND (1947–1960)

1980s Letter by Web Hanson to Fred Ireton on the Founding of the Guild

To: United States Bartenders' Association

From: Web Hanson, Young's Market Company

When I came back from the Navy in 1947 one of my first duties was to introduce Pimms Cup to So. California. Mr. Jack Finney, owner of Pimms Restaurant in London, came to Los Angeles to help do this. Mr. Finney, who was also Executive Secretary of the United Kingdom Bartenders' Guild, had been in touch with Angus Angerosa, the Head Bartender at Sterns Restaurant, about starting a Chapter of the Guild in Los Angeles. We met with Angus and a bartender from The Colonial and one from Tam O'Shanter and I offered The Pelican Club Bar at Young's Market Company as a future meeting place. The next meeting was held and recruits came in from The Tail of the Cock, Tom Bergins, The Windsor and several other restaurants and hotels. So the Southern California Chapter of United Kingdom Bartenders' Guild was born.

The first competition was held in the Pelican Club with about 12 bartenders and about double that number of guests. The winner, who was from the Colonial Restaurant - I can't recall his name, was presented with a gallon size Pimms mug that was silver plated and properly inscribed.

Another competition was held a year later and then two years later a special competition was put on by Brown-Forman at the Beverly Hills Hotel. All drinks featured Early Times. There were over thirty competitors and over two hundred guests at this event.

I am especially pleased to see the new growth of your association because you are the people who build brands.

I greatly regret not being with you today.

Web Hanson

You may find this of interest

Fred

A reproduction of the first patch worn by the four UKBG-USA West Coast Chapter Founders on a trip to London

The first logo of the UKBG-USA West Coast Chapter

The late 1930s and 40s were heavily impacted by World War II, which started in 1939. This period gave us a few interesting cocktails that made it through the test of time. Drinks like the *El Diablo*, the *Zombie*, both versions of the *Mai Tai*, and the *Moscow Mule*, all stemmed from this period.

Angus Angerosa was at the helm of *Stern's Famous BBQ* in Culver City and the connection between the UKBG in England, and the bartenders working in the US became more and more tight.

One of the most active UKBG members who stayed in touch with Angus was Jack P. Finney. Jack had been very involved in the UKBG since the early 1940s, as he represented the H.D. Davies & Co, a supporter of the Guild and the owner of Pimm's No.1 Cup.

In April 1946, Finney was elected as one of the two trustees of the UKBG different sources also claim that he was the executive secretary. He was also speculated to have been the owner of the Pimm's Restaurant in London.[18]

Sometime in 1947, while launching Pimm's No. 1 Cup liqueur in the States, Jack traveled to Southern California to visit Angus. The idea was also to take advantage of the trip to meet with the bartending community and discuss starting a chapter of the UKBG in California.

Consequently, a second trip by Jack was organized in 1948 where the UKBG-USA West Coast Chapter was born. The letter on page 31, written by Web Hanson from Young's Market in 1980, best explains how the event went down. The letter was provided to me by USBG Past President Fred Ireton, who had the foresight to save it.

The inaugural "board meeting" was held inside the *Pelican Club* of Young's Market. During the first few years the newly formed UKBG-USA West Coast Chapter organized occasional gatherings and patronized each other's bars. Things really ramped up three years later after their first social get-together with representatives from the UKBG was held in Los Angeles at the original Scandia restaurant.

The UKBG-USA West Coast Chapter had the same quality of cofounders that the UKBG had in 1934 when it was founded: It was hard to find any better people to lay the foundation for the Guild at that time. John Durlesser, Edward Nordsiek, Angus Angerosa, and Joe "Popo" Galsini were the "top dogs" of bartending on the west coast. They had a shared passion for great drinks, hospitality, and bartender unification.

Cocktail competitions and other guild activities started taking place; these events inevitably raised the bar by allowing new and experienced bartenders to measure their skills with international veterans of the craft. Right around this time, an East Coast chapter of the UKBG was founded, as well. It was based out of New York and its activities remain a bit enigmatic, as I have found nothing but a few mentions of its existence under the name of UKBG-USA East Coast Chapter. When I spoke to Brian Rea, who was actually a cofounder of this chapter, he didn't have much to say about it.

---

18. Email interview with Luca Rapetti on 12 Dec 2022.

Vintage Pimms No 1 ad found in the UKBG's *Bartender* Magazine, 1952

Part of the original UKBG West Coast USA group at the original *Scandia* restaurant

Margarita cocktail ad inspired by
John Durlesser

Historical Member - John Durlesser

One of the six bartenders who were in the picture that I mentioned in the Prologue of this book, and someone that gave me inspiration to write this story, was John Durlesser. His facial expression in the picture was clearly screaming passion, and I sensed it. What I obviously did not discover until months later was that he had a very important part in the guild's history and of the cocktail scene in general. John had been one of the top dogs of bartending on the west coast of the US from the 1940s through the 1960s.

John was a founding member of the UKBG-USA West Coast Bartenders' Guild and helped organize competitions while cultivating a great group of bartenders that he mentored and chaperoned to international cocktail events. He was the guild's very first president and remained active until his death, which occurred either in 1970, or in early 1971.

If we had a dollar for every version of the story that claims the creation of the Margarita cocktail, we would have enough money to drink daily margaritas without ever having to go to work. The more I read about it, the more my head spins. Not only are there several stories on how it was created, but there are different versions of each story creating dozens of variables. In addition to those stories, there's also the *El Picador* cocktail story that was found in Bill Tarling's *Café Royale Cocktail Book* from 1937 that adds more complexity to the story. Since it is completely possible that it was invented by multiple people in different times and locations, I refuse to put you through a whirlwind of legends surrounding its invention, except for one of them involving John Durlesser.

John Durlesser

John Durlesser was the head bartender of *McHenry's Tail O' the Cock* restaurant located on La Cienega Boulevard in Los Angeles during the 1940s and 1950s. There were not many restaurants in the Greater Los Angeles area at the time that were more popular than McHenry's was. The restaurant's lounge was nearly always full of affluent folks and Hollywood elites.

Vern Underwood, the president of a liquor distribution company called Young's Market, had been assigned the distribution rights to Jose Cuervo tequila. Sometime in 1955, *McHenry's Tail o' the Cock* was ordering more "Cuervo" than any other restaurant in California. Vern discovered that this was because John Durlesser had created a special drink for a lovely guest of the restaurant named Margarita (Margarita Sames according to some sources). The drink was comprised of tequila, Cointreau, and lime juice and was served up in a salt-rimmed cocktail glass. The Margarita cocktail was an immediate success and John even submitted it as a cocktail recipe in 1949 for the guild's cocktail competition; ironically, it placed third. Vern seized the opportunity of the drink's success by running full-page ads in national magazines featuring a portrait of the woman with the slogan, "Margarita, more than a girl's name." [19]

On a phone conversation I had in 2018 with renowned cocktail historian David Wondrich, he explained that while John Durlesser "may or may not have" invented it, it is very credible to believe that he was the "godfather" of the cocktail. He popularized it at his bar and that triggered the launching of the advertising campaign with the slogan.

The Guild has had a special relationship with the Margarita for over seven decades. Consider this: the 1937 *El Picador* cocktail was first published in UKBG founder Bill Tarling's book; in 1949, John Durlesser's Margarita was entered at a guild competition and in 1989, *Tommy's Margarita* was created by USBG San Francisco's cofounder, Julio Bermejo(P. 126).

1952 U.K.B.G. Cocktail Competition in London
Left to Right: John Durlesser, Charles Berner, Homer Harris

---

19. https://www.barandrestaurant.com/operations/search-la-sea-orita-margarita - Last accessed on 6 May 2023.

Sun-Kissed Margarita
A Riff on the 1940s Margarita Cocktail

BY TIFFANIE BARRIERE

My inspiration is from Israel Beal, Horrace Harroll, and David Stokes, all Black citrus farmers who helped change the course of the citrus farming heritage on the West Coast. *The Colored Citizen*, an African American run newspaper published in Redlands in 1905 and 1906, shared stories of citrus ranchers. Citrus has long been a natural and delicious flavor component to the cocktail scene and an amazing fruit to harvest for those in agriculture. From the hands of Black farmers, Mexican workers, and bartenders across the world, citrus has been emblematic and romanticized for beautifully balanced cocktails, like the Margarita.

SUN-KISSED MARGARITA

1¾ ounces / 50 mL blanco tequila
1 ounce / 30 mL unsweetened hibiscus tea
¾ ounce / 22½ mL fresh lime juice
¾ ounce / 22½ mL fresh orange juice
¾ ounce / 22½ mL agave nectar

Combine all in a cocktail shaker with ice and shake cold for 10 seconds. Fine strain over fresh ice. Garnish with a dehydrated lime wheel.

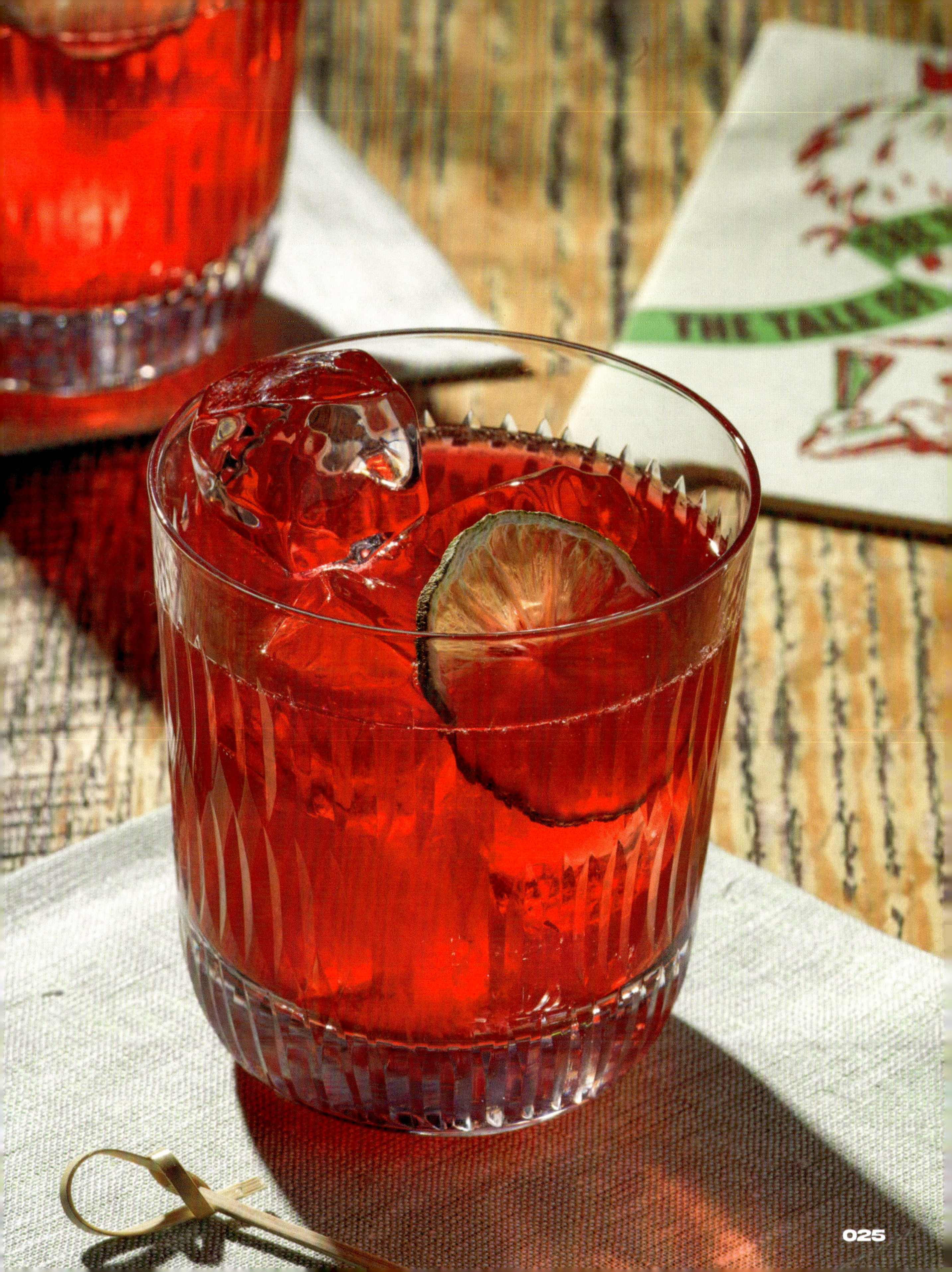

Luxury Cocktail #2
A Riff on the 1950s Luxury Cocktail

BY CHARLES JOLY

I have to admit, I had not heard of the 1951 *Luxury* cocktail (P. 125) before working on this project. I was pleasantly surprised by the unexpected ingredients brought together by Walter Simpson. Off the bat, the ingredient list read like something from a modern era cocktail list. Were people using much banana liqueur in 1951 outside of tiki? Who knows? I'd say Walter would be pleased to know that it had a resurgence amongst bartenders looking for a bit of levity in the late 2010s. His choice of herbal and bitter flavors is also perfectly in line with recipes of the past 15 years. More than a full-blown riff, I was inspired to re-jigger the original cocktail to what I see as working for the modern palate. The framework is all there, but the mid-century balance finished a bit abrasive and medicinal, in my humble opinion.

As with any classic, we don't know what we don't know. What type of liqueur was he using? What was the vermouth brand? How has the Pimm's recipe changed in the past 70 years?

The result of the *Luxury Cocktail #2* is bright, layered, and relatively complex. The banana, used judiciously, combines with herbs, fruit, bitter, and spice, yielding a result that walks the line between cocktail genres.

LUXURY COCKTAIL #2

1 ounce / 30 mL gin
¼ ounce / 7½ mL sweet vermouth
¼ ounce / 7½ mL banana liqueur
½ ounce / 15 mL Pimm's
½ ounce / 15 mL fresh lime juice
¼ ounce / 7½ mL simple syrup
2 dashes orange bitters

Combine all ingredients in a shake with ice. Shake and strain into a chilled coupe. Garnish: Mist with orange oils while cutting a twist with a channel knife. Curl and place twist on the rim of the glass.

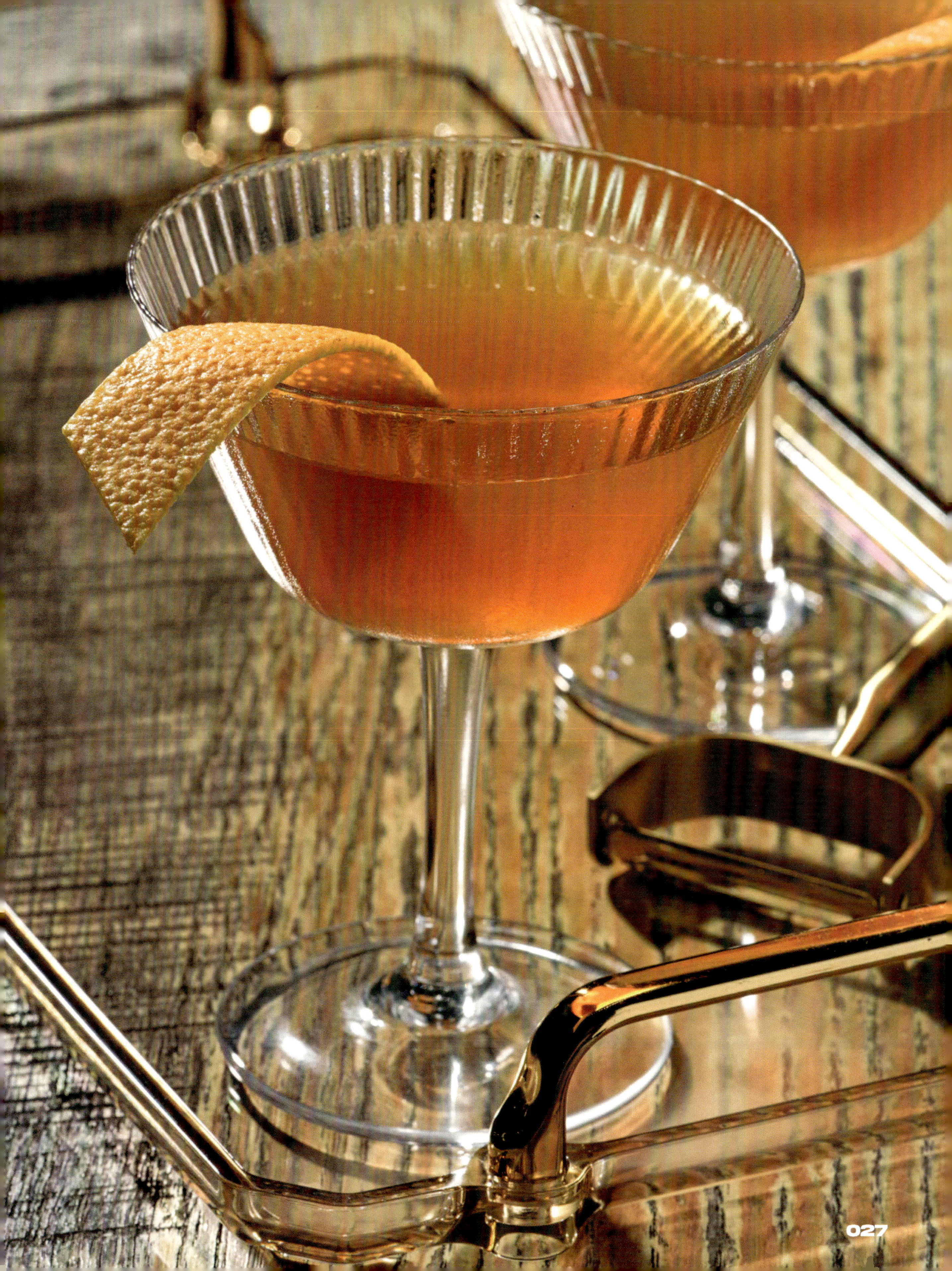

CHAPTER FOUR

GROWTH LEADS TO INDEPENDENCE: THE CALIFORNIA BARTENDERS' GUILD (1961–1971)

From Top, Left to Right:
Half page ad taken at a CBG-friendly bar
The Red Onion where Jose Ancona & Jose Ruiseco bartended;
1963 Souvenir program book;
A family affair with John and Charles Chop and spouses at the CBG's 1971 dinner dance event;
Judging at the National Cocktail Competition, 1969,
1969 Valentine's Charity Dinner Dance;
Two pictures capturing the CBG's 1971 dinner dance event

Red Onion
Sonora Style MEXICAN FOOD
COCKTAILS

BART EARLE
Sends Congratulations To
THE BARTENDERS' GUILD OF SOUTHERN CALIFORNIA
cbg MEMBER

And Best of Luck "To Our Bartender Members"
JOSE ANCONA — SAMMY MAYES — JOSE RUISECO

CALIFORNIA BARTENDERS GUILD

1962 Cocktail Competition

USA CBG West Coast

Ambassador Hotel — Monday, May 28, 1962

029

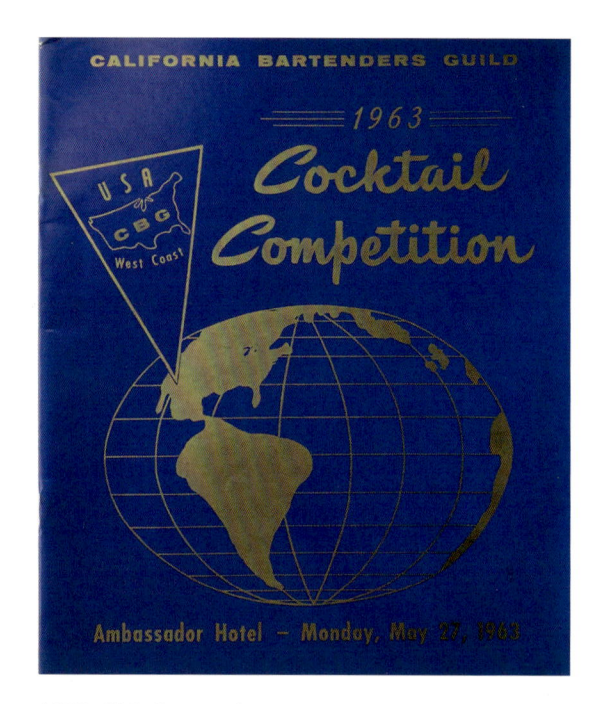

1963 CBG Souvenir program book

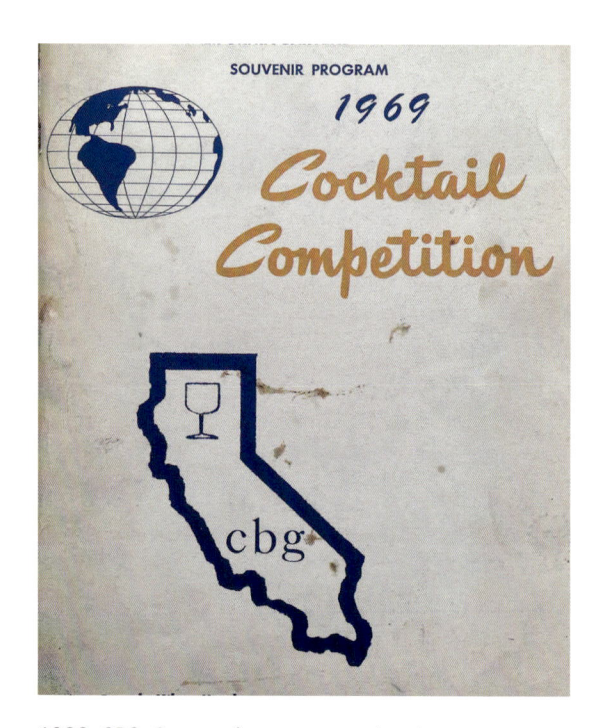

1969 CBG Souvenir program book

The years between 1960 to 1990ish are often grouped together and considered the darkest days of the American cocktail. Terms like the "Dark Ages," and "the death of the cocktail," are just a few that are used to define the drinks of this period. While different sources may cite slightly different start and end dates to this period, everyone agrees that these were terrible years to drink cocktails.

When interviewed in 2020, cocktail historian David Wondrich explained that in 1960s America, "Cocktails were struggling because they were kind of for the square, old-establishment types; they weren't for the new generation." He goes on by explaining that the old-school bartenders were retiring and getting replaced by people who were not going into it for a profession.[20]

As I was compiling this chapter, it became more and more clear to me that the trends of the Guild do not coincide with those of the bartending scene happening in America during the same period. This thirtyish year period for the Guild was very positive and full of highlights, and I have separated these three decades into two different eras.

The period that is traditionally referred to as the "Dark Ages" era of the American cocktail is divided into two different pivotal eras for the guild. One goes from 1961 to 1970 and the other from 1971 to 1989. This does not mean that the Guild and the "real world" were on two different planets; after all, Guild members at that time were working in the most respectable establishments of Southern California. What was happening in their bars was likely what was happening elsewhere in the country.

What was different was that they were not bartending on the side, they were professional bartenders. They had a deeper sense of belonging than your average bartender; they inspired each other and were mesmerized by the global bar scene, thanks to their affiliation with the UKBG. The UKBG was an affiliate of the *International Bartenders Association* (IBA) and, at that time, the IBA had over 20 affiliated Guilds across the globe.

By September 1961, the membership of the UKBG-USA West Coast Chapter had grown to about 100 members and 100 associate members. This allowed the group to petition the IBA to become a direct affiliate and no longer report through the UKBG. This petition was successful, and the California-based guild became the exclusive representative of the IBA in the United States. It changed its name to the California Bartenders' Guild (CBG) and, you had better believe, with that came new logos, crests, shields, pins, and all sorts of "swag."

This event further enriched the CBG members' sense of belonging. At the time, the organization reported to the UKBG. The winner of the national cocktail competition would go to England to compete in the UKBG cocktail competition. Now the winners would compete in the IBA finals that were (and still are) held in a different country every year. This motivated the CBG bartenders to train using international bartending techniques to compete overseas against bartenders from over 20 other countries. This allowed them to compare notes and learn from them as well.

The American bartender of that time, who was not as skilled as today's, gave the guests what they wanted, as the guild bartenders of the CBG did. They were not seeking celebrity status or

---

20. https://tulsaworld.com/drink-like-draper/article_dd7e4abc-1ff6-5ad1-b490-9602d484dfec.html - Last accessed 4/13/23

influence; they dished out hospitality through acts of service. Bar patrons requested fruity or creamy drinks that were bad, and the marketing of pre-packaged juices made them even worse, and the bartenders served their guests what they wanted without too much initiative in changing their drinking habits.

I would, however, be remiss if I didn't mention that a few of the drink recipes created by the CBG members during this era had validity and were well thought out. Examples of some of these drinks, that balanced fruity sweetness with spice and nuttiness, can be found in the recipe section of this book.

The CBG hosted several events at this time; they were geared towards socializing with the community and increasing the awareness of the cocktail. The monthly member luncheons with spouses and associate members from the liquor industry was a prime example of what to look forward to. This event allowed the distillers, importers, and distributors to rub elbows with the members of the CBG. It occasionally led to some CBG bartenders getting recruited by the liquor industry and pivoting their career paths.

A few other events to look forward to as a member were: the annual *Valentine's Charity Dinner-Dance* that was geared towards attracting spouses into the guild and raising money for charitable causes; and in November there was the employers and employees' event where members of the CBG would all break bread with their bosses and get the opportunity to meet their peers' employers. The yearly charity drive event further gave members a sense of inclusion and outreach. It raised money for the *Sky Ranch Foundation* and was a contribution that went on for nearly two decades.

The CBG was cool! Its influence was so strong that employers would take out full-page ads to brag about their staff member being a member of the CBG. Professional publications such as the *Beverage Bulletin* and the *Beverage Industry News* constantly followed the CBG to report the activities of its members.

Impactful "perpetual" trophies were created for the winning bartenders to display at their bars, and professional event program books were printed. These program books were the source of a lot of my information. As the Guild grew, it was also going through a generational change in leadership. Most of the OG members were still participating, but new leaders came into the picture. Lenny Casteel, John Chop, Fred Ireton, and Jose Ancona started to appear in the Guild rosters, and these folks would soon start lending a hand in enhancing the movement.

The Guild was a cultural melting pot. Having been founded by immigrants from different walks of life and having a direct affiliation to the IBA, it welcomed folks from all over. An example of its inclusionary spirit came from its several Filipino bartenders. They were met with arms wide open at a time when they were often unwelcomed in America. [21]

In November of 1967, to further incapsulate the importance of this era for the CGB, Popo Galsini won the *World Championship Team Prize* in Spain, and for the first time in the Guild's 20 years of history, it could add the designation "World Champions" to its name.

---

21. Melissa G. Flores, 2004. "Images from the Past: Stereotyping Filipino Immigrants in California https://core.ac.uk/download/pdf/72852287.pdf - Last accessed on 13 Apr 2023.

U.S.B.G. Perpetual Trophy — champions retained this trophy for one year to display in their place of employment

Souvenir cup offered in 1968 celebrating Popo's 1967 victory

Historical Member - Joe "Popo" Galsini: A Career in Tiki

José Valencia Galsini was born on the Philippine island of Luzon on March 19, 1900, or 1904. He came to America in 1928, through the port of San Francisco, and was apparently a schoolteacher prior to becoming a bartender. By 1941, he went by his iconic nickname "Popo," serving tropical drinks at the *Tropics*, an informal cocktail lounge in Hollywood.

In the 1930s and 1940s, Filipino bartenders were the backbone of tropical drink-making, and Popo became a quintessential example of the affinity that had developed between Filipino immigrants and Tiki cocktail culture. He soon became one of Southern California's elite bartenders and some of his employers would brag about having Popo Galsini work behind their bar by designing ads, matchboxes, napkins, and more with his name on them.

Most of the bars he worked at were tropical drink havens, including *Kelbo's*, a Hawaiian barbecue place in Los Angeles, and *The Islands*, a Polynesian restaurant in Phoenix. After working at a few non-Tiki-themed bars, he landed a job behind the stick at the *Hukilau Polynesian Lounge* in the *Captain's Inn* in Long Beach. He seemed to jump jobs a lot and in the early 1960s he became the lead bartender at *Outrigger*, a Tiki bar located inside the famous *Surf & Sand Hotel* in Laguna Beach. Most of his jobs stretched for about a two-year span before he moved on to the next place. In 1971, he went to work for the *Disneyland Hotel* in Anaheim, and just two years later, he helped open *Ambrosia* restaurant in Newport Beach. By 1964, he had moved to *Palms*, a tropical restaurant adjacent to a master complex in Anaheim. In 1966, he went to the *Kona Kai*, where he invented the *X-15 cocktail*, the precursor to what would become the famous *Saturn* cocktail (P. 121).

According to a conversation I had several years ago with then Guild historian Charles Chop, Popo was not part of the original pre-UKBG group of bartenders that got together in 1948, but he was a founding member present at the UKBG-USA

Joe "Popo" Galsini

West Coast inaugural meeting the year after. He remained an active cocktail competition competitor of the Guild while taking on some of the creative tasks, like serving as a photographer during Guild functions, and as cocktail recipe coordinator during cocktail competitions. In 1953, his *Petake*—included in the recipe section of this book with many more of his cocktails—won the *UKBG-USA West Coast Cocktail Competition*. This drink also shows up in some literature under the name *Pikake*, the probable reason for this is because cocktail competitors would often modify the drink recipe—and occasionally its name—when going from the national to the international phase of the competitions.

Popo's legacy cocktail—*the Saturn*—is his original *X-15* cocktail with a meaningful name change. As Jeff "Beachbum" Berry explains in his 2010 masterpiece, *Beachbum Berry REMIXED*, the drink was named after a jet designed by the *Douglas Aircraft Company* engineers who were Popo's bar patrons at the *Kona Kai*. After the tragic death of a test pilot in an X-15 crash, Popo changed its name to the Saturn. When he brought the drink to the IBA world finals in Mallorca, Spain, it was awarded with an obscure "Challenge Cup–Team Award." Today, the drink lives on as a "must-have" Tiki cocktail. You can find the recipe for the *Saturn* on page 121 in this book.

AWARD WINNING POPO

1952 (3rd) Oli Oli ★ 1953 (1st) Pikake ★ 1954 (1st) Berne, Switzerland, Blue Gardenia 1958 (2nd) Island's Cocktail ★ 1959 (3rd) Queen's Choice ★ 1962 (3rd) Surf and Sand 1963 (2nd) Lioness ★ 1966 (2nd) Blue Chip Award, Mosquito and Outstanding Bartender Award · 1971 (2nd) Top Popo ★ 1953 – 1958 Secretary U.K.G.B. West Coast ★ 1964 – 1965 C.B.G. Vice President ★ 1967 Member U.S. Team World Champions I.C.C. Majorca, Spain   1973 ?

U.S.B.G. MEMBER

A Very Special Salute to the Bartenders of the World

POPO GALSINI
Beverage Manager

GERIL MULLER
Proprietor

Ambrosia
A Formal Restaurant In The Classic Tradition
Five O One – Thirtieth Street, Newport Beach
(714) 673-0200

GEORGE RACHLEWIECZ
Chef de Cuisine

GOSTA MULLER
Proprietor

15

Star of Earth
A Riff on the 1960s Saturn Cocktail

BY MARTIN CATE

The *Saturn* has been a long favorite of mine, and first appeared on one of my menus in 2006 at the first bar I co-owned, *Forbidden Island*, in Alameda, California. At first, it was met with limited interest and the sales were quite low. There was some pressure to drop it from the menu, but a few die-hard regulars who loved it fought for it, and informally called themselves the "*Save the Saturn Society*." Eventually, its popularity spread, and it became a staple at all of my bars around the United States.

The *Star of Earth* was inspired by the discovery of a new ingredient, a rhubarb amaro called *Bing Zhou*, produced by a local San Francisco Bay Area company called Bitter Journey. Owner Richard Wei created a range of amaro inspired by his family's traditional Chinese herbal medicine business. Finding an application for this complex ingredient proved a challenge, but I thought that some tropical flavors would be a nice foil to the amaro. We found that the almond and passion fruit worked well, and so adding the amaro to the *Saturn* became the next experiment. But the gin didn't work with it, and a few more experiments revealed the perfect base spirit in *Plantation Stiggins' Fancy Pineapple Rum*. We called it the *Star of Earth*, the English translation of the Chinese word for Saturn. It's been a hit on the menu at *Smuggler's Cove* – many cocktail lovers today are interested in new ways to enjoy amaro and this one is definitely from outer space!

STAR OF EARTH

1½ ounces / 45 mL Plantation Stiggins' Fancy Pineapple Rum
¾ ounce / 22½ mL Bing Zhou (rhubarb amaro - substitute Zucca Rabarbaro if needed)
¾ ounce / 22½ mL fresh lemon juice
¼ ounce / 7½ mL passionfruit syrup
¼ ounce / 7½ mL orgeat syrup
¼ ounce / 7½ mL falernum

Add all the ingredients to a cocktail shaker. Add cubed ice and shake. Double strain into a chilled coupe.
Garnish with grated nutmeg and a floating mint leaf.

037

Historical Member - Jose F. Ancona: Holding Down the Fort

Jose Fernandez Ancona joined the California Bartenders Guild in 1965 after waiting five years for a spot to open (only 86 members were allowed at that time). He is gone, but never forgotten, as he was the heart and soul of the Guild for five decades. Jose bridged the gap between the Guild's "old" and the "new guard" in the late 90s. Throughout his many years as an active Guild member, he held many leadership roles, culminating with that of International Bartenders Association Vice President for North America, the highest-ranking position in the USBG.

As Jose stated in his Foreword to this book, we met in 1999 when I was tending bar in San Pedro, California. Jose welcomed me to the Guild by visiting me at the bar and relaying the message in person. It was one of the nicest things that could possibly happen to anybody who had just moved from a different country, as I had. At that time, the cocktail resurgence was slightly starting to edge its way up, with bartenders trying to move away from the cloying and colorful drinks that had been bar staples for 20-plus years. I was bartending at *Neil's Pasta & Seafood Grill*. "Neil's" was a family-oriented Italian restaurant, and even there, the guests couldn't resist ordering the "best" profanity-named drinks of the time.

Jose oversaw the international affairs of the Guild, and the rest of the IBA community knew that the US was not at the top of its cocktail game. Jose saw the cocktail resurgence coming and had the vision to put the US back on the IBA's map of great cocktails. He accomplished this in July 2001 by putting together a great team of three American bartenders to compete at the world finals of the *Bacardi-Martini Grand Prix* in Malaga, Spain.

Jose F. Ancona

While the details of that story will have to be for another time, the success of the US at that competition was massive. It was Jose's way of demonstrating to the IBA that America was coming back stronger than ever. It also inspired pride in the USBG, and our Guild saw a spike in creativity in the years immediately after that.

Jose created several cocktails during his tenure as a bartender for more than 56 years, but the 1971 USBG Cocktail, is such a perfect representation of his cocktail style. You can find the recipe for the *USBG Cocktail* on page 128 in this book.

What I Learned from Jose

When I first joined the USBG, Jose would often call me to chat about rejuvenating the Guild and how he wanted me to be at the center of the project, and I might have taken that too seriously. After the 2000s, as the cocktail scene continued to elevate, more USBG chapters were being founded and the Guild was both growing and rejuvenating. One day, Jose and I had a disagreement; the growth and rejuvenation mission he gave me took over my best judgement and became, at least in my mind, my only mission for the Guild. In the heat of a board meeting, I respectfully told Jose that his idea about adding another cocktail competition was not a good one, and the fact that the Guild was growing meant we were doing the right things. "The results speak clear," I said. Jose wisely replied, "Livio, the Guild is only growing if the love amongst our existing members is growing, and social gatherings help with that." This was the moment I realized what a massive heart Jose had and how he genuinely cared about his fellow Guild members, and not just about growing the Guild's membership.

Jose Ancona's entry for the USBG Cocktail

Jose Ancona loved clowns and enjoyed drawing them. He would donate his drawings to the Guild and they were raffled off at Guild events for fundraising. Jose had a big heart, he would visit foster kids and put on a big red clown nose to entertain them. During these visits he would also draw clowns for the kids.

Ancona Special
A Riff on the 1970s USBG Cocktail

BY JULIO CABRERA

I was inspired by legendary USBG member and, my dear friend, Jose Ancona. This drink is a variation of the original *USBG Cocktail* that Jose created in 1971 to celebrate a major milestone in the Guild's history.

The California Bartenders' Guild (CBG) was transitioning to a national organization and becoming the United States Bartenders Guild (USBG). The colors of the CBG were gold and blue but the transition to the USBG changed the colors of the Guild to bright red, white, and blue. As a result, the red jackets were launched as the guild's new uniform. This delicious red cocktail was Jose's idea to celebrate the milestone.

My variation is a style of drink that you would often see from Cuban Cantineros. It showcases that perfect blend of simplicity, freshness, and well-balanced ingredients.

ANCONA SPECIAL

1½ ounces / 45 mL Banks 7 Rum
½ ounce / 15 mL Benedictine liqueur
½ ounce / 15 mL raspberry syrup
¾ ounce / 22½ mL fresh lime juice

Add all the ingredients to a cocktail shaker. Add cubed ice and shake. Strain into a chilled coupe.

Garnish and aromatize with an orange zest.

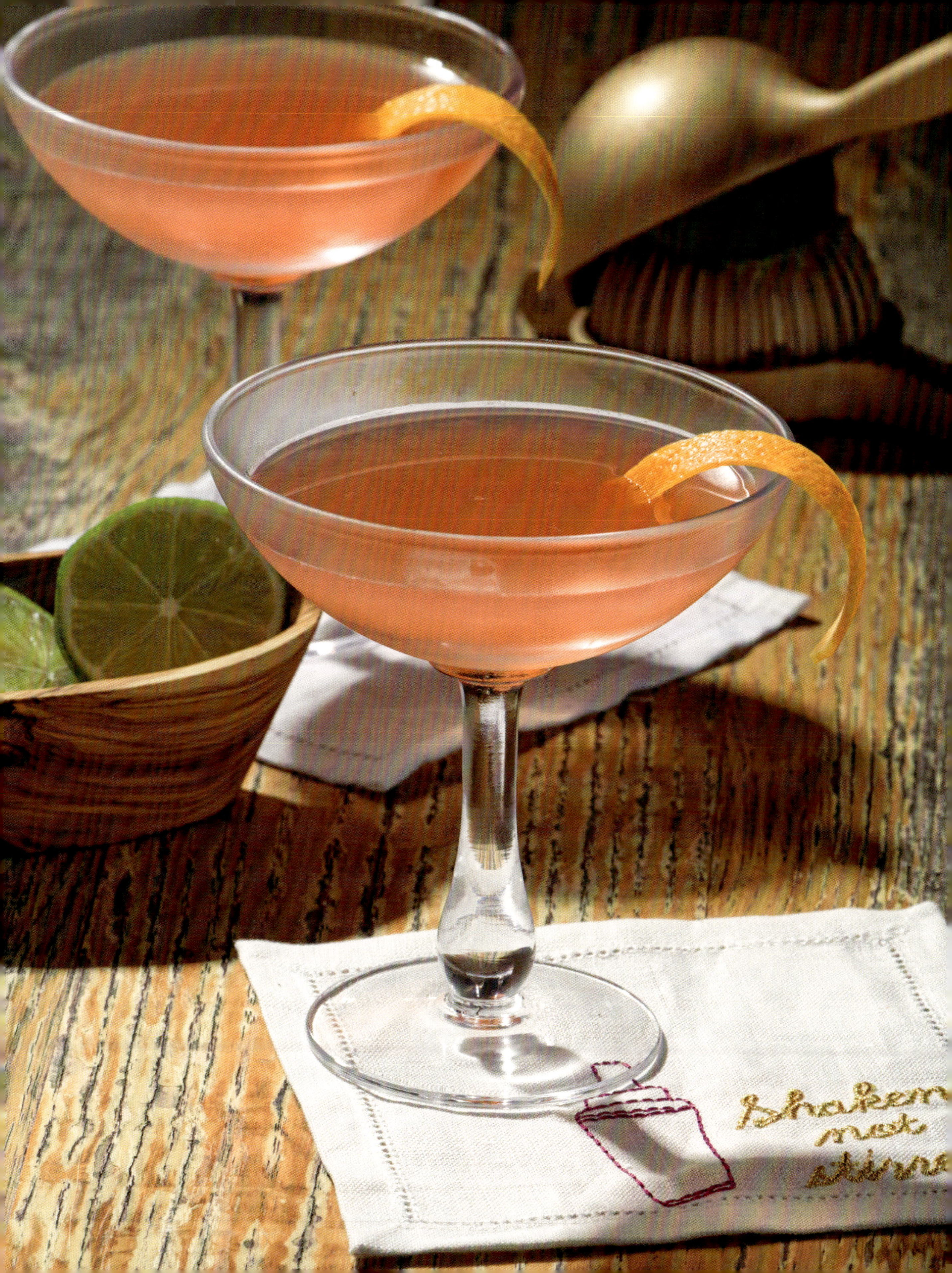
not

"The Guild is only growing if the love amongst our existing members is growing..."

Jose Ancona

Oil painting by Jose Ancona of a USBG pennant hanging on a wall surrounded by a red cocktail and bar tools.

Courtesy of Cody Ferguson
Photo by Bronson Loftin

043

CHAPTER FIVE

THE USBG AND ITS FIRST GOLDEN ERA (1971–1986)

From top, left to right:
Winners of the 1975 USBG National Cocktail Competition (from left to right: 2nd Place, John Rettino; 4th Place, Ray Swanson; USBG President, Charles J Chop; Grand Champion Bobby Batugo; Master of Ceremonies, Peter Zamuto; 3rd Place, David Stoker);
Bobby Batugo, shaking a cocktail 1975;
1973 Competition activities;
M. Stellar and C. McNeely;
Bobby Batugo's *"New Day"* Cocktail, 1973

Try a Prize Winner

Amaretto di Saronno · Originale · 1525

These two prize winning drinks garnered top honors at the 33rd Annual National Cocktail Competition of the U.S. Bartenders Guild.

"New Day"
recipe by Valerio "Bobby" Batugo

1½ oz. Vodka
¾ oz. Amaretto di Saronno
⅜ oz. Melon Liqueur
2 oz. Orange Juice
½ oz. Roses Lime Juice

Stir, pour over crushed ice, float with melon liqueur.

USBG pennant used to display at bars

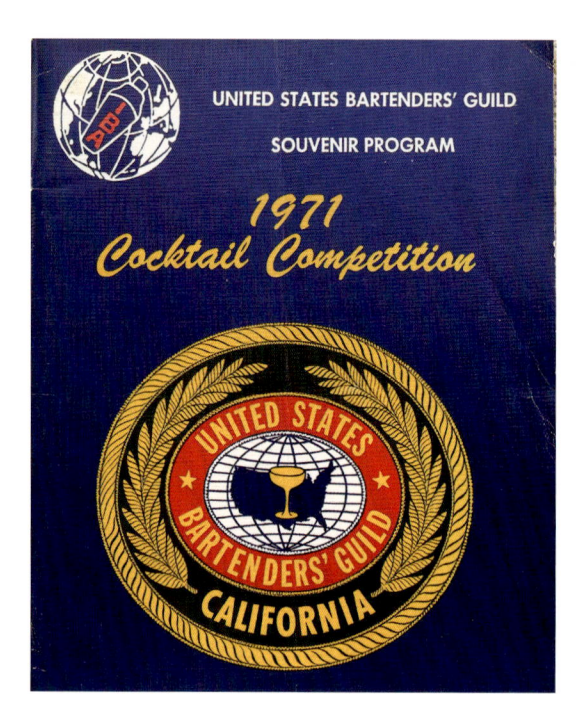

1971 USBG Souvenir program book

Stamped filing of the USBG's Articles of Incorporation dated August 31, 1971

Throughout the 1960s, the CBG and its members grew more and more influential. CBG bartenders were serving movie stars, models, and average Joes in some of the best bars of the time.

This era was easy to trace back because the cocktail competition program books of the Guild provided a yearly update under the title of "Cameo Happenings," and they spelled out the Guild's activities and the lives of the Guild members.

The mixology skills of the Guild members were superior. At a time when synthetic emulsifiers, fake juices, and sugar bomb ingredients were the norm, CBG members were showcasing craft cocktails. Thomas Malta only pressed fresh juices. Virgel Jones only used fresh egg whites to emulsify his cocktails, even though synthetic versions were the norm (and sponsors of the Guild). Leroy Charon would add a few dashes of Pernod into his sour-style cocktails to add an extra level of complexity. James Campbell mixed his own coconut pineapple juices, despite bottled colada mixes readily available and sponsoring the Guild. Jose C. Yatco was dishing out solid tiki drinks at the China Trader in Burbank.

The sad ingredients of this era that were overly used by the Guild were heavy cream and Half & Half; they were often added into drinks that had no business including them.

On the other hand, so many of the frowned upon vodka drinks of this era often made by CBG bartenders were crafted with more depth than what was out there. One day, Jose Ancona and I were drinking Negronis, and he explained to me that Guild members usually used two liqueurs when mixing with vodka. One of them would have an herbal, piney, or rooty component, and was used with the intent to make the vodka more interesting, while the other liqueur was used as the alcoholic modifier of the drink.

Bobby Batugo used Licor 43 in vodka in his drink, Hank Wirstuk (P. 085) used Damiana liqueur, Anthony Giacco (P. 114) used Strega, Kurt Behringer (P. 127) and Phillip Cormier (P. 080) used both a combination of Galliano and Grand Marnier. Several of these drinks showcased more complexity than the usual vodka drink of the time.

USBG legacy member Charles "Charlie" Chop

Time to Grow Up

The growth in membership, and perhaps some motivational pep talks from the IBA and the liquor industry, brought the demand for the CBG to expand to more states across the country. This propelled the transition to becoming a national organization.

In August of 1971, the United States Bartenders' Guild (USBG) was officially incorporated as a nonprofit corporation to respond to the need of a nationwide bartenders' Guild. It assumed the exclusive charter from the IBA as its sole USA affiliate.

The USBG operated the same way as the CBG with all the existing events and activities developed by the CBG. Part of its innovation included establishing a bi-annual blood bank for its members and loved ones. Bartender innovation at this time meant "let's make our lives better," a trend we have seen in recent years, too, where health and safety are big topics at major bartending events. The USBG also established a membership relief program. Records show that in 1974, the family of the late Guild member Richie Pozo, received $255 to help with his burial costs. The Guild was family!

Under the leadership of President Leonard "Lenny" Casteel, a bright future seemed the only predictable outcome for the Guild. Lenny was a charismatic person who had attended several IBA International Cocktail Competitions (ICC) over the years. These gatherings had always been hosted overseas by other IBA affiliates. They brought USBG members to Tokyo, Stockholm, Copenhagen, and St. Vincent to name a few. Meeting minutes show that Lenny had a deep desire to host an ICC in America one day.

Local cocktail competitions were very well organized and detailed, and every member participated in a specific role in addition to competing. The judges were mostly women and attendees from the crowd. To keep a consistent path and bridge the gap of generational changes, all past presidents of the Guild would attend the events.

In 1985 Kelly Lightner becomes the USBG's first African-American National Champion. His cocktail, the *Malibu Orchid*, is featured on page 106 of this book.

These years were very entertaining for the members and the excitement was passionately documented by Charles "Charlie" Chop, a legacy member I had the pleasure to meet in the early 2000s. Charlie loved to write, and his recaps made my job of writing this book a lot easier. He documented the international camaraderie of that time, embellishing the prestigious image of the Guild. He bragged about the USBG Sunday brunch events for members and spouses, the Seagram's-sponsored lunches, and a plethora of important guest speakers from different walks of life at guild events.

1980s era USBG lapel pins

The ICC in Los Angeles

President Lenny Casteel and his leadership team worked with the IBA and proposed to host the 1973 ICC in Los Angeles. The proposal was accepted! In November of 1973, five hundred people from the bartending community of 26 countries came to Los Angeles to celebrate the Country's first ICC. The ICC today is called the WCC (World Cocktail Competition) and is still the foremost cocktail competition in the world with over 50 countries participating. This was a time when just about everything the Guild touched turned into success. It was the most successful era of the Guild.

Hawaii Chapter

On June 22, 1981, the Hawaii chapter was founded; this exciting group of bartenders had a very strong potential and backing. The mayor, the governor of Hawaii, *Hawaii's Visitor's Bureau*, *Hawaii's Hotel Association*, and 22 associate members from the liquor industry, all showed support to the new chapter of the Guild. The Hawaii chapter was, "mixologically speaking," very talented. They showed very little interest in pre-packaged products and put forth fresh tropical cocktails that were both beautiful and delicious.

Florida Chapter

In 1983, the Florida chapter was inaugurated with 47 members right out of the gate. This chapter was founded by legendary bartender Santiago "Pichin" Policastro. The Florida chapter was very hospitality-driven and mostly inspired by the Latin-American flair of its founders. The cocktails from the bartenders are tied into the tropical climate of the southern end of the state.

A Nightcap At Kaimana Beach
A Riff on the 1980s Nightcap Cocktail

BY JEN ACKRILL

In 1965, *Top of Waikiki* opened as one of the tallest buildings on *Kalakaua Avenue* in the heart of Waikiki. It was the place to see and be seen. Celebrities and regular folks alike from Asia and the US Mainland took the slow, wood paneled elevator up 18 floors and then two escalators to the twentieth floor of the Waikiki Business Plaza. If they were without a much sought after reservation, they would have been escorted up three more tiers of the circular restaurant to the "top of the cake". Here they would find a sunken bar, with a top that revolved around the stationary barmen who were crafting $.95 Manhattans and Whiskey Sours while local musicians played classic Hawaiian songs peppered with modern hits from Don Ho, Elvis Presley, and Moe Keale.

In 1983, Rositito "Tito" Ledda was one of those barmen in the sunken *Top of Waikiki* Bar with guests revolving around his workstation. Here he created his *Night Cap Cocktail* (P. 111), with gin, falernum, grenadine, fresh orange juice, Dole pineapple juice, and a classic 80's orange wheel as well as a bright maraschino cherry garnish. Mr. Ledda won the 1983 USBG Hawaii Chapter Long Drink Competition with his tropical creation, no doubt hoping to rise to Hawaiian cocktail fame like Harry Yee, the creator of the classic Hawaiian favorites: the *Tropical Itch, Banana Daiquiri,* and *Blue Hawaii.*

And now 40 years later, I am honored to have been asked to reinterpret Tito's drink, because in 2014, I moved to the bustling city of Honolulu to helm the bar program at that very same Top of Waikiki where Mr. Ledda created his winning cocktail. At first glance, to modernize the drink, it just needed a little acid to balance out the sweetness, but I wanted to have some fun and make a truly nightcap cocktail using Tito's ingredients as inspiration. Keeping with the original vibe of the drink, I started with gin, but felt that with grenadine and falernum in the mix, I could really do something fun and funky with St. George Terroir gin. Then taking a nod from the pineapple juice, I reached for the *Plantation Stiggins' Pineapple Rum* and continued with Tito's lead using *Geijer Spirits Falernum* and *Liquid Alchemist's* rich grenadine. To tie in the orange juice ingredient, I added *Regan's* orange bitters, and then my favorite citrus peel, the grapefruit, as the garnish, finishing the drink with pretty pink, floral, and citrus notes. I love this drink and hope that another generation in another time from this beautiful island gets to use the *Nightcap at Kaimana Beach* to inspire them to create their own USBG cocktail.

A NIGHTCAP AT KAIMANA BEACH

1 ounce / 30 mL St George Terroir gin
1 ounce / 30 mL Plantation Stiggins' Fancy Pineapple Rum
½ ounce / 15 mL Geijer Spirits falernum
¼ ounce / 7 ½ mL Liquid Alchemist grenadine
3 dashes Regan's orange bitters

Add ice, stir, and pour into a Nick and Nora glass.

Express and garnish with a manicured grapefruit peel.

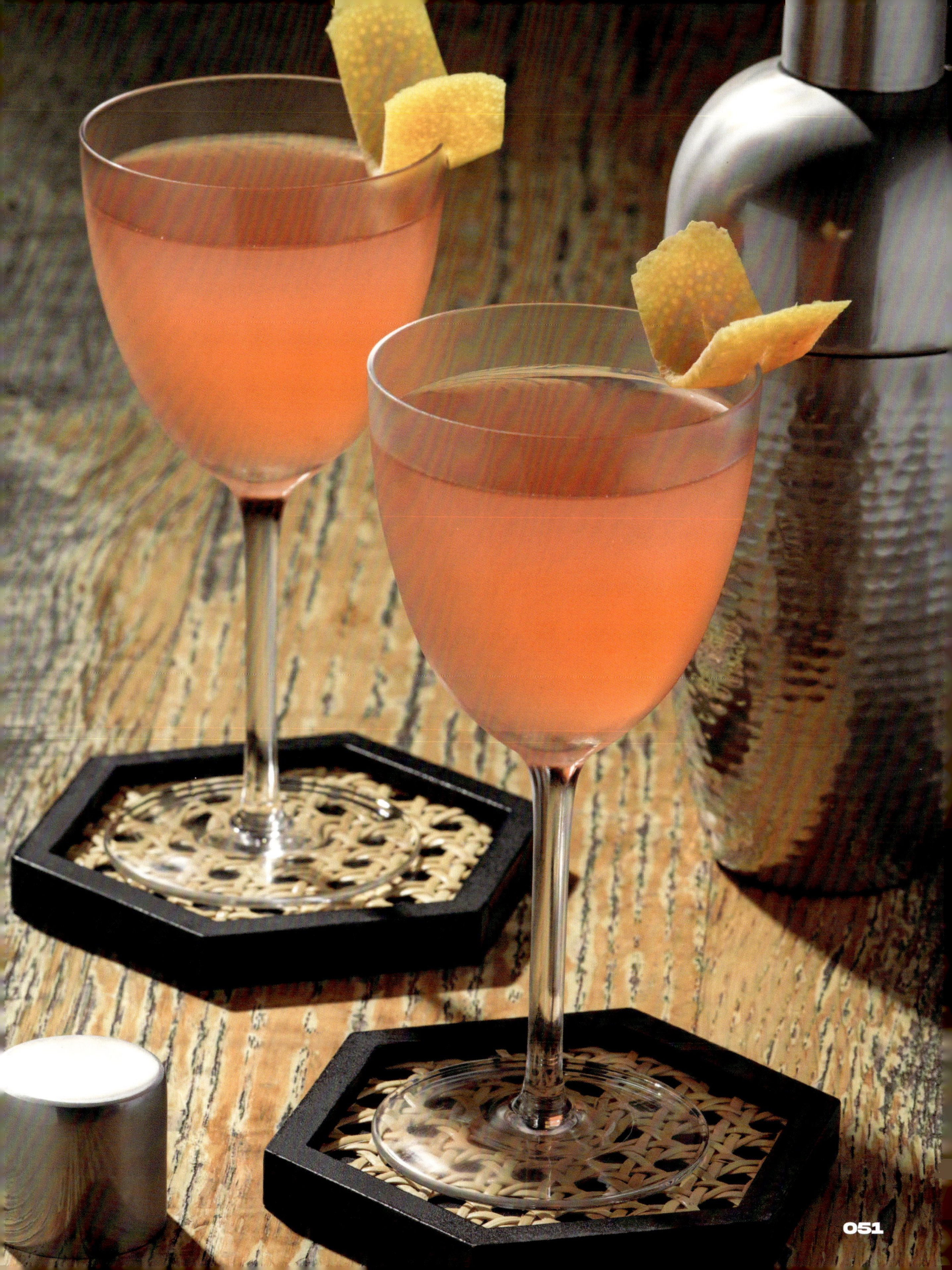

CHAPTER SIX

THE WTF HAPPENED ERA (1986–1999)

From Top, Left to Right:
Cocktail Competition snippet, 1987;
Four Awarded bartenders at the National Cocktail Competition, 1990;
Francesco Lafranconi's First *Academy of Spirits* picture, 2000;
USBA Logo, 1986;
Two Awarded bartenders at the National Cocktail Competition, 1990;
Francesco Lafranconi, Shirlee Pisano, Jose Ancona, 2001;
Tony Abou-Ganim Making Holiday Cocktails at Bellagio Hotel Las Vegas, 2001;
Colorful Long Drinks from the IBA World Finals, 1995;
Charles Chop, Naomi Filburn, Virgel Jones, Vince Cisneros, Fred Ireton, 1996

Champion

053

Marina Del Rey T.G.I. Friday's, 1985

Cocktail (Film), 1988

When the Guild transitioned to a national organization in 1971, the goal was to spread its wings and recruit new bartenders from across the country. As I wrote in the previous chapter, this had come to fruition thanks to the founding of the Hawaii and Florida chapters. Entering the mid-1980s, those chapters gave the illusion that the Guild was growing, but after just a few years of excitement, things changed; both of those chapters dissolved and resulted in short-lived endeavors. By 1988, the Guild was left with one chapter again in Southern California, and it had fewer members than had been seen for at least two decades.

The founding of the chapter in Puerto Rico also played into the illusion of growth for the USBG. It brought a breath of fresh air to the Guild. This chapter was simply an in-kind gesture from the USBG to help establish an independent Guild in Puerto Rico. It was like how the UKBG lent a hand creating a Guild in the US back in 1948. After two years, Puerto Rico was able to become a direct affiliate of the IBA and no longer needed to report to the USBG. In 1989, the Illinois chapter was founded with seven members and, just like the Hawaii and Florida chapters, they were out of the picture the following year.

An Aging Guild

Have you ever had that feeling that something strange is about to happen even though there are no indications to back it up? That feeling might make you more alert about a potential curveball coming your way. Well, I wish somebody from the Guild would have had that feeling, as it could have changed the course of USBG's history.

The 90s was a polarizing cocktail era; most of the bars still served mediocre at best drinks, and if you were a bartender during these times, you were, almost inevitably, doing the same. Guild bartenders carried themselves as experts in their craft. They were career classic-style bartenders, a dying breed at the time. The drinks that came from their hands were crafted to the liking of their guests and to the taste of that era.

When I first joined the USBG as an overseas member in 1998 and learned more about it, I wondered, "How could a group of bartenders who built such an important legacy, watch it slowly crumble in front of their very eyes and not be able to do anything about it?" The USBG was something that took a lot of work to create. It involved decades of consistent passion for a craft that was mostly underappreciated. Letting it deteriorate and watching it go from its glory days to the "Dark Ages" is something so hard to fathom; especially when considering that America was going through an age of rediscovering cocktails.[22] When taking a closer look, it doesn't take an expert in "bartender guildology" to see that while the Guild was on top of its game, and enjoying its illusion of having a national footprint, its members were getting older.

As the industry was changing and bartending was adapting to the times, the guild was not; it found itself in a deep ditch by 1986. When I analyzed the literature, meeting minutes, and newsletters of the organization, I realized that the reason for this downfall had been staring at me the whole time: The members were getting older and subsequently retiring, while no new blood

---

22. https://www.chanticleersociety.org/index.php?title=Cocktail_Timeline - Last accessed on 13 Apr 2023.

was coming in. So many members had worked hard throughout the years to get the guild to its highest point, and now the time had come for them to let go of the hustle, have some drinks together, and enjoy the camaraderie. From a social aspect within the Guild, this just might have been the best era. Members ate, drank, and were merry! For this reason, the aging of the Guild was being internally celebrated.

The USBG's bartending style, mostly dictated by the IBA cocktail competition rules, was an old-school style of making drinks that was far more celebrated overseas than in America. But the Guild stuck to its guns, and the new era bartenders in t-shirts was not something the leaders of the time knew how to appeal to.

The Guild started carving out space in their newsletter for what was called the "Nostalgia Corner," highlighting pictures and events of the past when the members were young. The Cameo Happenings section of the newsletter had become more about the "good ole days," rather than recently joined members. The updates published by the Guild included info like: "Our member J. Popo Galsini is now the world's youngest senior citizen." This over-celebration of the past was fueled by the fact that there wasn't much of the present to brag about.

The death of the classically dressed bartender contributed to this decline, too. A new lifestyle had impactfully edged its way in. The 1980s brought with it an attire that was much more casual and brighter. The colors were big, and life was more cheerful. Stylish people wore very bright-colored clothes, Hollywood movies were very colorful, and anything in neon was trendy. Not many young bartenders wanted to associate with older folks wearing outdated clothes at a time when brighter things were happening. Despite the red jacket as the Guild uniform, the perception of the USBG was not one of youthfulness, and this put a burden on recruiting new members.

The Guild made some interesting, and out of touch, attempts to create awareness. One was to change the name from "Guild" to "association." The thought process was that the term was more approachable. After several heated debates, the name was officially changed in 1986 to the *USBA*. This endeavor failed to work, and by 1989, the organization's name had reverted back to *USBG*.

By the late 1980s, the total membership was only 40 members, half of which were retired senior citizens enjoying the camaraderie they had worked so hard to build.

Staying Classic While Going Flair Helped

During these dark times of the Guild's history, the organization strove to maintain its internationally classic style, while somewhat reluctantly welcoming the flair bartending community. On a global scale, the IBA nurtured a network of both classic and flair bartender members and the USBG's affiliation with the IBA benefited from this.

---

23. Phone interview with Tobin Ellis on 20 Apr 2023.

A few flair bartenders joined the Guild in the late 90s; they were hipper, younger, and what the USBG needed. They were mixing the contemporary-style cocktails of the time and were a breath of fresh air. As quintessential prize fighters with a deep interest in competing and winning, they made the competitions far more interesting with their acrobatic skills and high energy.

The generational gap between the USBG's leadership team and most of the new young members of this period made it hard for the Guild to hold their interest, and most of these new members would sign up for one year only to never renew again.[23] What the struggling Guild was mostly in need of to survive were folks that would be willing to help pick it up again. Enter the era of "ask yourself what you can do for the Guild, not what the guild can do for you."

A Respectful Nod to the Past

I am not going to attempt to name every member, associate member, employer, and bar patron who helped the USBG become what it was during the glory days. It would be a daunting list and I would get so much of it wrong. I have, however, added a *Wall of Honor* with the names of the USBG members from the old guard who had the foresight to start the guild and keep it alive during the "Dark Ages" and before the year 2000. They receive nothing but my respect because they donated their time and money in keeping the USBG afloat at a time when bartending was not cool, and the guild was not cool... Respect!

Teeing Up a Revolution

America is the third largest country in the world by both area and population. By default, it is not an easy ship to turn. There are vastly different realities that exist city by city and state by state. These different realities often give birth to conflicting historical trends being reported.

I toured Southern California for over a month in 1998 to visit relatives and learn more about the world of cocktails. I visited Hollywood, Santa Monica, Sunset Boulevard, Pasadena, Downtown Los Angeles, Long Beach, San Pedro, and several of the other beautiful beach cities of the area. I was already a very observant bartender at the time and couldn't find the craft cocktails resurgence that a few other cities claim to have started as early as 1985. Not that it wasn't happening, it was just nowhere to be seen.

Dale DeGroff

As a classically trained Italian bartender, I was taught the craft as a discipline, so I did find it fascinating how flair bartending worked in some of the bars doing it at the time. Flair bartending was less discrete and drew all the attention to the bartender. It was different from how I had been taught the craft and could fit perfectly when properly implemented. From a classic cocktail bar standpoint, there was very little for me to learn and bring back to Italy, where I was already mixing up most of the classics.

Therefore, from my Southern California-based lens, in the late 1990s, the classic cocktail scene needed a revolution. That revolution came and the hospitality experts in America were able to turn that ship. The era pertaining to this revolution starts after the timeline of this book, which is intended to cover the first 50 years of the guild, a period which ends in the year 1998.

As I mentioned earlier in this book: during all historical moments of gloom in the history of bartending, there are consistently some great things building up yet invisible to the naked eye. Hindsight is always 20/20, so the following questions should be easy to answer now, and were nearly impossible to foresee at the time:

- In the 1990s, could the cocktail scene in America make a 180 degree turn for the better?
- Could bartending become a respected profession again?
- And lastly, could the USBG attract bartenders who would care enough about being members of the guild and bring it back to a place of respect? The resounding answer to those questions is YES! YES! YES! YES!

The revolution involved several moving parts that are not within the scope of this work, but there were some impactful things that happened to the guild.

In 1997, Robert Hess, a cocktail enthusiast who worked for Microsoft, was researching valid resources for cocktail recipes. At that time, there were few resources available online. It didn't take him long to realize that the bartenders of that day had lost their way, so he started learning from the few books he could find. As he was digging into his cocktail research, he ran into the fact that there was an organization called the United States Bartenders' Guild. He eventually came across an email address and reached out to Fred Ireton. Robert Hess would go on to assist USBG with its website for over a decade alongside managing his own iconic cocktail portal by the name of Drinkboy.com. Drinkboy was one of the first websites to provide insights on craft cocktails.

In 1990, a bartender by the name of Dale Degroff became a member of the guild. Dale went against the grain of the times and was at ground zero of the cocktail revolution. In 1987, he was the opening bartender of

Tony Abou-Ganim

---

24. Phone interview with Dale Degroff on 21 Apr 2023.

the *Rainbow Room* in New York, creating epicurean-influenced cocktails with fresh citrus and premium ice cubes that were considered a novelty at the time.

Dale previously lived in Southern California from 1978 through 1984, working as a bartender, while trying to become a professional actor. It was during this time that he became acquainted with the USBG. When he joined in 1990, Dale's influence on the guild, and the craft cocktail movement, revolutionized the cocktail scene for decades to come.[24]

In 1996, Tony Abou-Ganim, a 36-year-old bartender from *Harry Denton's Starlight Room* in San Francisco joined the guild. He, too, had aspired to be an actor in years prior; once he made bartending his chosen profession, he went looking for a bartender community.

Google searches were not an option at the time, but he was lucky enough to stumble on some literature of the "unknown" USBG. He joined the guild and started attending their meetings and competitions. Tony genuinely enjoyed his first endeavors with the older guild members, who made him feel like family, and in Tony's words, "They shared the liquor from the flask they brought to the event generously."

Tony had an unmistakable desire to promote craft cocktails, something he had been inspired by when visiting the *Rainbow Room* in New York City to drink a Negroni at Dale Degroff's bar. That flamed orange peel garnish ignited a flame in Tony, too!

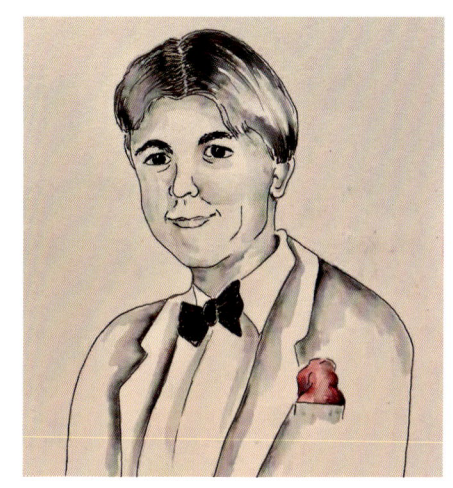

Francesco Lafranconi

In 1998, Tony was selected to develop the cocktail program for the new *Bellagio Resort* and Casino in Las Vegas. He relocated from San Francisco to Las Vegas and implemented a philosophy of bartending that had never been seen before on a large scale. Most experienced operators thought he was crazy when he insisted that the drinks were to be made with fresh juice pressed in-house daily at a high-volume casino. His ability to prove that fresh ingredients and premium bartending could be done in the resort's 22 bars was a gamechanger in the industry. Suddenly the term "it makes no sense to do that" started to make no sense.[25]

Just one year later, a young and enthusiastic barman from Italy, Francesco Lafranconi, visited Las Vegas to test the waters. He had been recruited to start an academy for bartenders sponsored by *Southern Wine & Spirits*, with the mission to elevate the craft and professionalism of bartenders. His trip to Las Vegas gave positive vibes, so he went back to Italy, packed his bags, and moved to Vegas the following year to start the *Academy of Spirits and Fine Service*.[26]

The impact these three USBG members had on the organization, along with so many other colleagues from the cocktail community, would prove to be massive! But that, my friends, is going to be for another day.

---

25. Phone interview with Tony Abou-Ganim on 21 Apr 2023.
26. Phone interview with Francesco Lafranconi on 21 Apr 2023.

Historical Member - Bobby Batugo

When I was born my dad was 52 years of age and my mom was 30 years old. My dad kept himself young and in relatively good shape as my mom did, but he was also very jovial and young at heart. He was born in 1920 and always lived in the present until the day he passed away in 2016. Growing up at home with parents having such a different age gap was often unnoticeable. My dad lived a very rich life rooted in family, food, wine, friends, and just the right amount of nostalgia. That nostalgia was ingrained in the happy moments of the present and you could just feel it in the air. The great marketing guru Seth Godin would likely say that my dad "learned how to dance" with his nostalgia.

Compiling the *Liquid Legacy* has been one of the most fascinating projects in my life. Sifting through information and hunting for facts allowed me to immerse myself in the people I am writing about with an occasional daydream about what happened on a specific day. Often my facial expression would change when the characters changed. I have the same reaction when I read my dad's very fun autobiography book. My assumption is that growing up in a happy household that knew how to dance with its nostalgia taught me to have a deep appreciation for the past, especially the years that follow my dad's birth.

By far the most fascinating character in the history of the USBG is Bobby Batugo. A young Filipino bartender who lived a full life.

Bobby was born Valerio Gamet Batugo on April 26, 1906, and he emigrated to the US in 1926. He worked in a sawmill in Washington State and saved money to buy a bus ticket to Hollywood. Once in Hollywood he was hired as a busboy at *Henry's*, a restaurant on Hollywood Boulevard financed by Charlie Chaplin when it first opened, circa 1930. Henry's had the distinction of being the first Hollywood restaurant to stay open after midnight. In an interview with the *LA Times* in 1985, Bobby recalled that Charlie Chaplin was very nice to him but could not pronounce his name. One day, with the help of Bobby and the rest of the waitstaff at *Henry's*, they chose to start calling him "Bobby" and that name stuck for the rest of his life. Bobby Batugo sounds so Hollywood !

Bobby had dreams of becoming a prizefighter so when he wasn't working at the restaurant, he was boxing in the gym. He moonlighted as a boxer for seven years and even fought to a draw for the California

Bobby Batugo

championship. In the same interview with the *LA Times* Bobby tugged on his ears while laughing and said, "Seven years fighting and no cauliflower ear. I'm not punch-drunk. I had some talent."

It was in 1932, during Prohibition, that Batugo got his first job as a bartender in a speakeasy. He was not at ease about making a living illegally, but loved to be around people. His big personality made bartending come naturally to him. When in December, 1933, Prohibition was repealed and bartending became legal, Bobby decided to go all in on the profession.

He became a high-profile bartender working in some of Hollywood's most exclusive clubs. One of those was *Sardi's* in Hollywood, a celebrity-packed restaurant that was opened in 1932. There, he landed a role on the morning radio show, *Breakfast at Sardi's*, one of the most popular shows at the time. For eight years in the 1930s and 1940s he traveled the country with the show, performing a bartending-comedy routine for a national audience. Bobby claims that he traveled everywhere with the show, and that is how he learned every drink in America.

In 1948, Bobby was working at the private *Key Club*, an exclusive lounge located in *Café La Maze* on Sunset Boulevard, when he was recruited by restaurant operator Tip Jardine to go to work at a small restaurant and coffee shop in Valencia called *Tip's*. The job at *Tip's* Restaurant was not the kind of place that Bobby was used to working at. It was not glamourous and the venue itself, as defined by the great Tiki scholar Jeff "Beachbum" Berry, looked a bit like "a *Denny's*, with a bar alongside it." However, Bobby looked beyond the surface and saw something very appealing in it—artistic freedom. Tip told Bobby that he could experiment with exotic drinks as often as he wanted. He gave Bobby an unlimited budget to buy any product he wanted. The job was so great he ended up working at *Tip's* for decades. For Bobby, there was more to bartending than serving classics; he preferred to ask guests what product they like and would make a drink for them. He would name the drink after that person and write down the recipe to make the drink consistently the same anytime they came back to *Tip's* and ordered it. Bobby elevated mixology to levels not previously seen in the area, attracting all the legal drinking age folks of the area. It was a watering hole with a legit cocktail culture. Salesmen from around the globe would go to *Tip's* to ask him to create a drink with their product.

Bobby was an active member of the USBG participating at all major events and recruiting new members including his very own nephew, Mario. His name appears on several USBG cocktail competition committees demonstrating that, even in the later years of his life, he showed up to work and not just to compete and socialize. Bobby won the USBG national cocktail competition three times with drinks like *Best Year* (P. 095), *Memmories* (P. 107), and *Universe* (P. 128). Several of his drinks are celebrated by bartenders today and are included in the recipe section of this book.

Did Bobby Serve James Dean His Last Drink?

A As I was reading up on *Tip's* Restaurant in Santa Clarita, where the talented Bobby Batugo worked, I came across a story that put me through a tangent which I am happy to share with you. I was checking if there were any more drinks that Bobby might have created while working there to include in the recipe section of this book.

Tip's offered a sizeable selection of items for breakfast, lunch, and dinner along with an array of beverages from coffee to alcohol and cocktails served by Bobby himself. I also learned that there were two locations of *Tip's* operating simultaneously that were just a few miles apart in Santa Clarita. The first *Tip's* was at Castaic Junction (where Bobby worked) and the second the second was *Tip's Coffee Shop*.

I then came across a story covering the last moments of the life of the young James Dean. The story didn't pertain to anything I am writing about, but I kept reading. The 24-year-old actor died in a car accident at 5:45 PM on September 30, 1955, in Cholame, California, when the Porsche 550 Spyder he was driving hit a Ford Tudor sedan at an intersection.

The story I read—and several others—traced back his journey that day and claims that he made a stop at *Tip's* before getting back into his car and getting into that accident just two hours later. This piqued my interest to understand if perhaps the movie star had stopped by *Tip's* to order a drink from Bobby, a thought that isn't too far-fetched knowing Bobby's past in serving Hollywood elites.

Althea McGuinness, a *Tip's* waitress who died in the 1970s, was reported to have served Dean at the restaurant on that tragic day. Despite her testimony and that of her manager stating that James Dean was there, there is one fact that still points to him potentially not making that stop. I believe he was, because I have trust in the observance skills of restaurant people. Nonetheless, James Dean's last meal at Tip's, according to the testimony, was pie and milk, so Bobby did not serve him before his deadly accident.[31]

> "Guests never forget me. That makes my job a pleasure. I love to be loved and I love 'em all."
>
> **Bobby Batugo**

Bobby Batugo (1982 national champion) and his nephew Mario (1982 national champion) at Tip's restaurant

---

31. https://scvhistory.com/scvhistory/pollack1108jamesdean.htm. Last accessed on 4 May 2023.

063

USBG WALL
DEDICATED TO THE LIQUID LEGACY

Al Arteaga	Edward F. Nordsiek
Al Conklin	Edward D. O'Brien
Alfredo Fontana	Edward Hutchison
Albert Repetty	Egidio "Angus" Angerosa
Al Swinney	Emilio Rodriguez
Andrew Pawlak	Fredrick A. Boyd
Anthony "Buddy" Giacco	Fred Brown
Armando Vasquez	Fred Ireton
Arturo A. Peinado	Gay Wayman
Benny Supnet	George Borella
Bob Watson	George Sperdakos
Bobby Batugo	Ike Cabalar
Brian Rea	Irvin B. Frost
Brian Tamashiro	James "Jimmy" P. Campbell
Carole Bodene	Jimmy Jones
Cathy Cisneros	José "Popo" Galsini
Champ Clark	John Baltazar
Charles J. Chop	John C. Burton
Claire L. Reed	John W. Chop
Clayton H.Q. Tom	John A. Rettino
Collin L. Bullard	John Schmidt
Dan O'Shea	John Durlesser
Dick Sansone	Jose F. Ancona
Earl Takasaki	Jose Manzano

OF HONOR
RESERVED BY PAST MEMBERS OF THE USBG

Jose Ruiseco
Judy Johnson
Kathleen Bodnar
Kelly Lightner
Kenneth Decker
Kurt Behringer
Leonard "Lenny" Casteel
Lyle H. Gordon
Max De La Fuente
Max Lynch
Milt Silverman
Naomi Filburn
Nick Beehler
Nick Kitchupolos
Nicholas Kotsonas
Noreen Wood
Norman Toon
Peter Zamuto
Phillip Cormier
Phil Kirros
Philo Miller
Ralph Bisbois
Raymond Foat
Rick Supnet

Ricky Takahashi
Robert G. Iverson
Robert H. Weall
Robert "Bob" Watson
Rudy Caberto
Russell Muncy
Sam K.Y. Ho
Sam Rovner
Sean Dukerich
Shirlee Pisano
Smith Lowther
Rositito "Tito" Ledda
Tom Malta
Tom Stenger
Tony Zangari
Vince Cisneros
Vincent Giuliani
Virgel Jones
Walter Coleman
Wes Dodd
William Bradford
William "Bill" Brown
William Messmer

The Urban Transit
A Modern Riff on the 90s Cable Car Cocktail

BY BRIDGET ALBERT

This drink is a tribute to my friend Tony Abou-Ganim's *Cable Car* cocktail (P. 085). It is inspired by the bustling city life and creativity of today's bartenders. It features a blend of flavors that resonate with contemporary palates, showcasing innovative techniques and unique ingredients.

THE URBAN TRANSIT

1¾ ounces / 50 mL orange infused rum*
½ ounce / 15 mL Aperol
¾ ounce / 22½ mL fresh lemon juice
1 ounce / 30 mL simple syrup
4 dashes Old Forester Smoked Cinnamon Bitters

Shake all ingredients, except bitters, with ice, and strain into a chilled coupe glass.

Garnish with 4 dashes of Old Forester Smoked Cinnamon Bitters and a lemon twist.

*Orange Infused Rum Recipe
1 bottle (750 ml) unaged rum
4 large oranges
3 vanilla beans
4 cinnamon sticks
½ cup super fine sugar

1 Wash oranges. Using a peeler, carefully remove the zest from the oranges, avoiding the bitter white pith.
Place the orange zest into a clean glass jar with a lid.
2 Split vanilla beans lengthwise and scrape out the seeds using the back of a knife. Add the vanilla seeds and empty vanilla pods to the jar with the orange zest.
3 Add cinnamon sticks and super fine sugar to the jar.
4 Pour rum over the ingredients in the jar, making sure they are fully submerged.
5 Seal the jar tightly and give the jar a good shake.
6 Place the jar in a cool, dark space and let it infuse for up to a week, shaking the jar once a day to help the flavors to meld.
7 After the desired infused time, strain the rum through a fine mesh strainer into a clean bottle or container, discarding the solids.

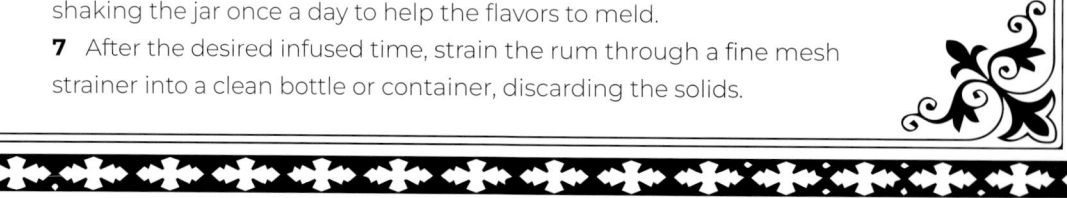

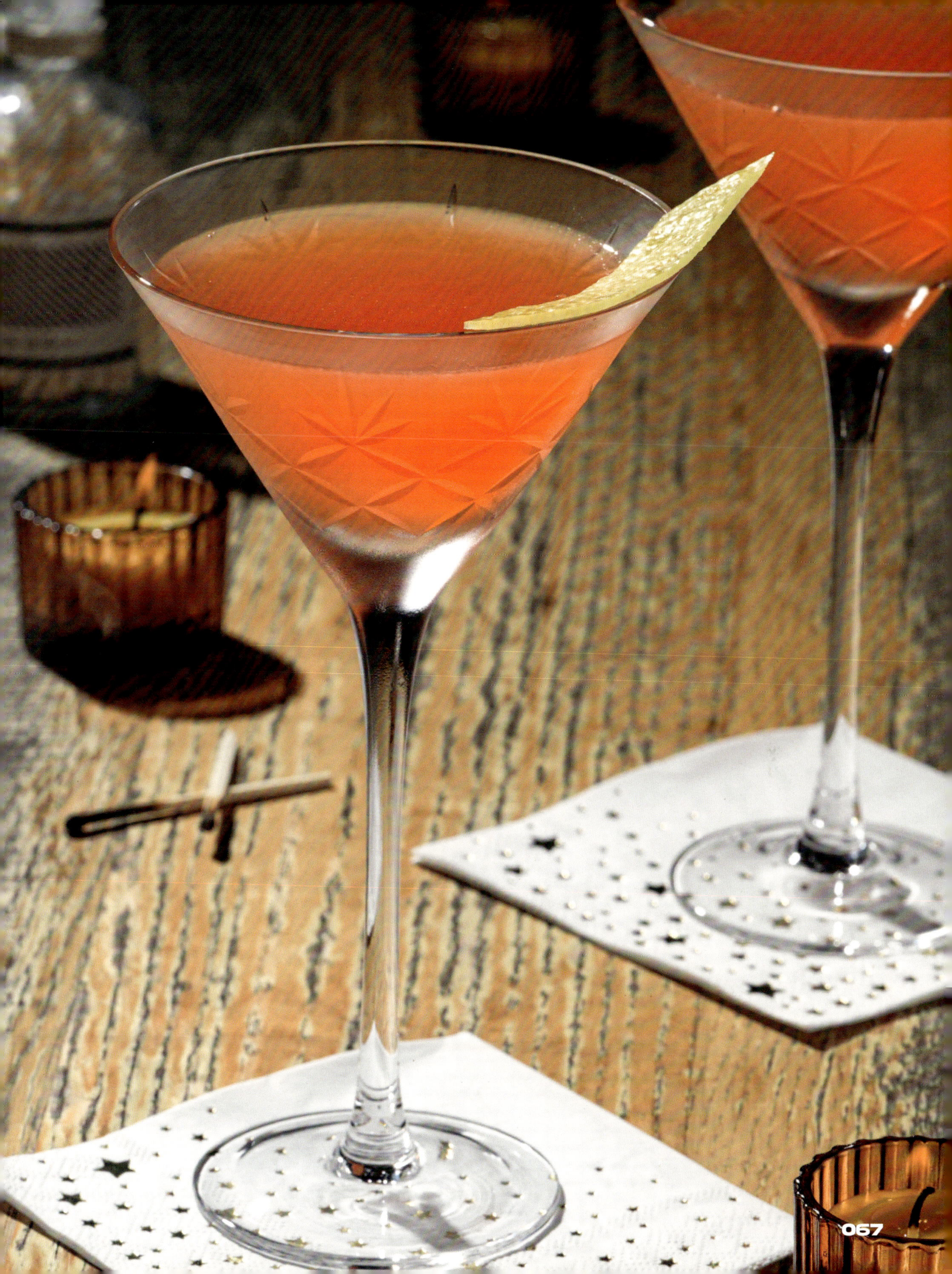

Historical Member - Fred Ireton Successfully Bartending Sober for 55 Years

Fred Ireton was born in Kansas City, Kansas, on April 26, 1934, and moved with his family to Pasadena, CA, at the age of six. He spent most of his early childhood in Pasadena, before moving to Fontana, CA, where he grew up playing and working in an orange grove. Fred graduated from *Chaffey High School* in Ontario, CA, and attended *Chaffey Junior College* in Rancho Cucamonga, CA.

In the mid-1950s Fred began a career in public relations for several title insurance companies, and a big part of his job was to entertain clients and associates with food and drinks. This is when Fred's love for alcohol and cocktails began. He started drinking so much that his excess drinking became the reason for which he would find himself frequently without a job.

In 1965, he became a bartender. His first job was at a friend's restaurant in San Bernardino, where he would help watch the bar while his friend was out for errands. Fred was a natural for bartending, and his charming personality and ability to quickly learn how to mix drinks showcased the talent needed for his new profession. [27]

Through the years, he would end up working at various restaurants and bars and at one point landed a great bartending position at the *Arrowhead Country Club*. It was a place he enjoyed working at, as he stated when I visited him in spring of 2023. However, being in the business of serving alcohol, his drinking problems constantly threatened to end his bartending career as well. Fred continued losing jobs, and sometime in the mid-70s, he reached rock bottom. He recalled attending several *Alcoholics Anonymous* meetings, but never finishing all the steps before starting to drink again. Fred went on, explaining that sometime in 1979, he checked into the former *Long Beach General Hospital*, where he completed the 90-day rehabilitation program. This event changed his life. At first, he lived in a halfway house for a year, and eventually got another bartending job, yet Fred never had another drop of alcohol again. [28]

From 1980 to 1988, Fred bartended at the Santa Ana Elks Lodge, where he met his wife Patty, and became one of the most recognized bartenders of his time. Fred won two back-to-back USBG national championships in 1990 and 1991, and those two victories

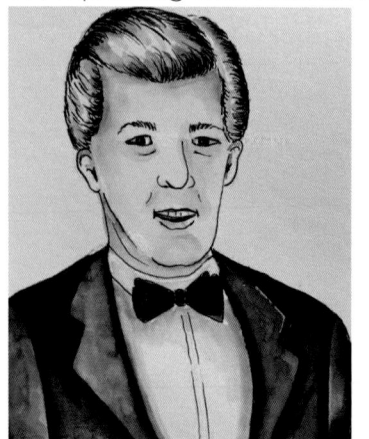

Fred Ireton

---

27. Phone interview with Fred Ireton on 18 Apr 2023.
28. https://www.latimes.com/archives/la-xpm-1997-05-19-me-60198-story.html - Last accessed on 9 May 2023.

brought Fred to represent the US twice at the International Cocktail Competition. In 1993, he was elected to the *Bartender Hall of Fame* and served two terms as national president of the USBG in the late 1990s.

Fred's biggest accomplishment came from being a respected and sober bartender for over 55 years. When I met Fred, I could not wait to ask him how he knew that his drinks were worthy of being presented in national and international competitions if he had never tasted them. He responded by explaining that he had a group of brutally honest women who he called his "drink committee." They were not shy about telling him how bad his drink was, and he would tweak it until they liked it. Fred's drink committee was the first of its kind and resulted in Fred winning roughly 15 awards without tasting a single drink.

Fred recalls becoming a better bartender once sober, because he could spot if any of his guests were on the path of over drinking beforehand. He told me, "Before that, I was half in the bag myself." He took on the responsibility of promoting responsible drinking and would frequently speak at *Alcoholics Anonymous* meetings to inspire those who were going through what he had in years prior.

You can find several of Fred's committee-critiqued cocktails in the recipe section of this book, keeping in mind that palates have dramatically changed since the 1980s and 1990s.

Historical Member – Naomi Filburn: How Women Forged the Guild

Much of my information gathering of the United States Bartenders' Guild's history was not obtained in chronological order. As one can imagine, the more recent the event, the easier it was to come across information. When I started putting together the puzzle, I had several pieces from the 1980s and 1990s; and not much from the 1940s through 1970s.

For this reason, my early search results gave light to the fact that the Guild's activities always included women at the most important events. Of course, they attended the competitions, galas, charity events, and gatherings, but they were also included as judges, Person of the Year recipients, and council members. If cocktail competition judges were as important then as they are today, then the female palate and integrity was likely highly trusted, as most of the judges were women. Equally as important was the "Person of the Year" award: an honor given during a ceremony that highlighted the achievements of somebody who had offered a valuable contribution in the industry. That person then gave a speech at the gala and received a full-page feature in the Guild's program book.

In 1980, USBG President Anthony "Buddy" Giacco made it very clear how important it was to bring in more women, by including more inclusive language in the program book, and proudly recognizing three new female bartenders who had recently joined the California chapter. In 1988, the council unanimously voted Associate Member Carmen Smith, from the *Paddington Corporation*, Person of the Year. I believe she was the first woman to win the award since it was founded in 1976. In 1990, Marsha Roberts, a USBA associate member, was given the same award.

In 1988, the Guild made an important step forward by electing Gay Wayman to the council. She was the first woman council member I was able to find documentation of, and she was seated at the table with Bobby Batugo, Charles Chop, Fred Ireton, and a few more council members of the time, to help shape the Guild's direction. I could not come across any women competing in cocktail competitions prior to 1987, when USBG member Carole Bodene from the *Revere House* competed.

Naomi Filburn

---

29. https://www.inc.com/damon-brown/the-surprisingly-revolutionary-battle-for-women-to-bartend.html. Last accessed on 6 May 2023.

The State of California did not allow women to bartend until May of 1971 when its supreme court overruled the discriminatory law, but things still moved very slowly after that. There was a section of that law forbidding women from serving beer from a fixed bar, which wasn't removed until 1976.[29] At that point, the rise of women in the industry was quick, and by the end of the 1980s, women represented the majority of bartenders in America.[30]

The advent of women competing in the Guild's cocktail competitions took its time. Internationally, the IBA started accepting women members in 1975, with female competitors trickling in slowly. By the time women could start competing, the overly rigid rules of the competitions had not yet adapted to how bartending had changed with the times. This further deterred several men and women. The male-dominated competitions remained stale until Naomi Filburn entered the scene.

Naomi is a bartender who worked at Hollywood Park Racetrack for over 30 years. She also held a second job as bartender and server at the Anaheim Convention Center where she still works to this day. You can also find her at the Los Angeles Coliseum making drinks for thirsty thrill-seekers from all over the world.

In the 1990's Naomi also tended bar at the Beverly Hilton Hotel which is where she met USBG member and four-time national champion Caesar Sandoval. Caesar invited her to join the Guild, so she did.

She is not just an expert in the game; she is also one who does not get easily discouraged. Naomi started competing in 1996, and her demeanor screamed confidence; this became very encouraging for the men and women present. She also became a USBG council member in 1997 and encouraged all the women of the Guild to be bolder while trying to get younger members to join. Accompanied by "Macho," her loyal Pomeranian, she was a breath of fresh air at a time when the USBG was truly struggling.

Naomi's signature cocktail is the *Zinger* (P. 129). It's a whisky drink with herbal, anise, and vanilla flavors. She submitted the recipe in 1988 with Suntory "Old Whisky," Galliano, and a hint of lime cordial. In 2016, under the leadership of President David Nepove, she was honored by the USBG with a *Lifetime Member Award*.

> **"Even though I was one of the few women members at the time I joined, the men were always encouraging and congenial which is an important part of being a bartender and a USBG member."**
>
> **Naomi Filburn**

---

30. https://daily.jstor.org/how-women-fought-for-the-right-to-be-bartenders/. Last accessed on 6 May 2023.

John Burton and Brian Rea
Teaching Cocktail Techniques

I am speculating a bit here, but to be a head bartender at a cutting-edge bar in the 1970s and 1980s it would have been sufficient to be properly educated in a few basic, time-tested essentials. The first would be to learn the duties and tasks of the bartender; this would include a checklist of things to do before, during, and after your shift along with sanitation and responsible service practices. The second would be basic alcohol product knowledge; and the third would be basic cocktail-mixing techniques. How about that? No sou vide needed, no tinctures to be made, and no instagrammable cocktail making skills required!

Today, those three time-tested essentials make a solid base for a future cutting-edge bartender to build from. Most of the Guild bartenders from the last two decades of the twentieth century had that same basic level of cocktail skills; they knew the essentials. They showed marginal interest in drinks education while displaying far more interest in the social aspect and the sense of belonging that the USBG had to offer. I don't find anything wrong with that, and this is exactly why Guilds and associations have loyal followers. A few members were interested in taking their knowledge to the next level; some collected vintage cocktail books and were knowledgeable of the teachings that came from the pioneering bartenders of their past. As a matter of fact, Fred Ireton owned a respectable collection of books, and he often enjoyed implementing what they taught during his younger years. Other members also collected old cocktail books, and the info contained in those pre-Prohibition publications would be posted in the Guild's newsletters from the 1970s on.

The newsletter was like the monthly bible for the Guild, so posting that type of info would go a long way for the readers. More education came from a few Guild members who would go to work for liquor companies. They became modern day brand ambassadors. These members included Angus Angerosa, Thomas Stenger, Lenny Casteel, and John Durlesser. They were a hybrid between a sales rep and a bartender schmoozer and would offer product education to the Guild until the mid-1980s. In the 1990s, things changed, as those

John Burton & Brian Rea

education-driven members and ambassadors were retiring and there was very little educational effort in the Guild that I could find. This trend continued until Brian Rea and John Burton entered the scene.

Brian and John created a newsletter called *BAR*, which was dedicated to the beverage community. Both Brian and John were two of the largest vintage cocktail book collectors and drink historians of the time. The acronym *BAR* stood for "Burton and Rea." Their newsletters and roadshows covered several topics pertaining to spirits, cocktails, hospitality, and bartending. The duo put on a smart and witty show and made education fun. Brian died in 2020. In a recent interview with John Burton, he remembers Brian's unique way of teaching with a fun note of humor in his tone, but if you were distracted or disruptive in class, Brian would make you regret it.

John Burton was born in San Francisco, CA in 1939. He became a professional bartender in 1959 and enjoyed a long career operating his own catering business, concessions stand, bartending school, and much more. In the late 1980s he would be appointed by USBG President Fred Ireton to bring education initiatives back to the Guild. John kickstarted that slow process even though the Guild's small membership base did not give his initiatives the broad audience it deserved.

The educational efforts for the Guild took another step forward in the late 1990s, when Brian and John started publishing the *BAR* newsletter. In it, you would find all sorts of information, from basic to nerdy. Perhaps, next to an article on how to fill an ice bin, there would be a picture of Harry Johnson's preferred workbench, as seen in his 1888 book edition; that combination of coupling a basic bartending function with something the history junkies would enjoy united bartenders from different walks of life. John currently lives in Santa Rosa, CA. He played an integral role in the founding of the USBG San Francisco Chapter in the early 2000s.

Brian Rea was a veteran bartender turned author and teacher. He started bartending in 1942, and his career culminated with his position as the head bartender of the iconic *21 Club* in New York. After decades behind the bar, he shifted his focus to teaching, consulting, and conducting bar management programs for *UCLA* and *Cal Poly University*, as well as the *National Restaurant Association*. Brian's rare collection of cocktail books was the most extensive in the world before he sold it.

Brian cofounded the short lived and mystery-shrouded UKBG-USA East Coast chapter that appears in the U.K.B.G.'s 1953 issue of *The Bartender*. The representative on record for that chapter was William "Bill" Raymond, who Brian knew well, and I regret not asking Brian to tell me more about him.

EPILOGUE

To write a book about the USBG's first 50 years on its 75th anniversary leaves out a third of its history; so, I'd like to fill in a few gaps here. I'll start by saying that the 25-year span of history that lies outside the scope of this book has been so eventful that it would take a full set of encyclopedias to cover it; so, maybe I'm exaggerating, but you get my point! Throughout this book, I have done my best to explain the history of the guild, and how its journey fits within the realities of life outside the organization. This is because the USBG community is an active part of the greater bar community. Therefore, I am going to use the same process here.

America's "cocktail rediscovery era" of the 1990s progressively turned into a "cocktail restoration era," with drink quality and bartending skills reaching the same levels as they were during pre-Prohibition America. From there, it has progressed even further to a "cocktails are better than ever before" era. Almost concurrent to that timeline, the guild's success has reached its "better than ever before" era as well, and that is the present. A slight variation to the path of the greater bartending scene occurred due to a few big hurdles the guild had to jump over in the early 2000s.

I'll tease you with some real archive tidbits here to further stress how tough these hurdles were:

> This guild is in very, very deep trouble, and I feel that there is nowhere left for it to go.

> ...vious to me that we should forego this year's ... Competition. We just don't have the money ...ver to pull it off. So far, no money has been ...contract's signed. We can always appoint a me... ...esent us at the I.C.C.

In 2005, the guild started its own restoration, straightened up its finances, and teed up for the present. A lot more has happened since then, and today the USBG enjoys a true national footprint, with more than 40 chapters across the country, an ever-growing membership, and a key role in the cocktail revival. The USBG has played a major role in our country's growth in bartending skills and cocktail quality. Today, the USBG is that place where thousands of bartenders from all walks of life have come together to better their skills, share their thoughts, and support the industry as a whole.

Throughout this book-writing journey, and especially now that I am typing this last page, I have been hoping that the outcome of my writing is to give these past members their due credit. Most of them I have never met, but they have become like family to me. I love them because I adore those who fight for what they believe in, even when it is invisible to others. The guild meant the world to them, and they fought, scratched, and clawed to get it to where it is today; because of that, they are my heroes. I am sure to have missed some folks who did not surface in my research; so, if you know any of them, please point them out to the USBG, because I love them, too!

IBU ORCHID
(IMP. MALIBU)
BERRY JUICE OCEAN SPRAY
EAPPLE JUICE
EAT SYRUP (TEPP
UEEZE FRESH

AL REPETTY
"GREEN EYES"
1 oz. Pampero Rum - ANEJO PAMP
Melon Liqueur - MIDORI
apple Juice - DO
Creme -

Valerio 'Bobby' Batugo
MEMORIES
¼ oz. Amaretto (Di Saronno)
1 oz. Bailey's (Irish Cream)
½ oz. Blue Curacao (DeKuyper)
1 Drop Fresh Lemon Juice
2 Drops Frothee

1990
ed Ireton
TY BREEZE
White Chocolate Liqueur
arta Strawberry Margar
aspberry Schnapps
1 oz. Cream
ash of Frothee
with Whole Strawberry

"PRINCESS"
Jose Ancona
Build:
1 oz. BACARDI® rum
3/4 oz. Creme de Banana
Dash Grenadine
Fill with Orange Juice
Garnish with orange peel,
cherry & mint

1970 CHAMPION
JOSE C. RUISECO
"BANANA'S BREEZE"
1 oz. Christian Bros. Brandy
¼ oz. Bols Apricot Brandy
¾ oz. Bols Creme de Banana
1½ oz. Fresh Orange Juice

NATIONAL COMPETITION WINNERS

Al Arteaga	1976	Road Runner
Al Carrillo	1954 / 1958	Frosty Dawn / Honeymoon
Albin Farley	1957	Scotch Frog
Albert J. Repetty	1972 / 1974	Kool Banana / Velvet Kiss
Bobby Batugo	1975 / 1978	The Best Year / The Universe
Caesar Sandoval	1980 / 1987 / 1992 / 1997	Special Lady / Chona's Dream / Jo Jo's Best / Cecil's Dream
Charles Berner	1950	Bernice
Charles J. Chop	1994	By Pass
Edward F. Nordsiek	1952	Ed's Baby
Fred Ireton	1990 / 1991	Misty Breeze / Summer Breeze
Fructuoso Prado	1999	Ariana's Dream
George Kim	1984	Candlelight Dream
Jack T. Sherwood	1988	M'Adorable
José "Popo" Galsini	1953 / 1967	Petake / Saturn
John W. Chop	1977 / 1983	Chop Nut / Mellonaire
John Durlesser	1963	Kim
Jose F. Ancona	1989 / 1993	Princess / Flamingo
Jose Rusieco	1970 / 1998	Banana's Breeze / Conga Line
Jose C. Yatco	1969	Golden Wave
Kelly Lightner	1985	Malibu Orchid
Kurt Behringer	1966	Auburn
Leroy Charon	1959 / 1962	Golden Dream / Golden Amber
Mario Batugo	1981	Blue Heaven
Nicholas Kotsonas	1968	Satin Glow
Nick Beehler	1960	Evenings Delight
Peter Zamuto	1955 / 1964	Golden Comet / Tuacian
Robert G. Iverson	1996	The Winner
Rositito "Tito" Ledda	1983	Night Cap
Russell Muncy	1986	By The Pool
Tom Stenger	1956	Merry K
Tony Cordero	1973	Cognac Perino
Vince Cisneros	1995	Malibu Slide
Virgel Jones	1971	Cracklin Rosie
Walter Simpson	1951	Luxury
Wells Wescott	1979	Honey Bea
William "Bill" Brown	1965	Lulu

RECIPES FROM PAST GUILD MEMBERS

The following cocktails are recipes from the past. Some are good, some are great, and others represent lessons we can learn from. I have tried my best to leave no cocktails behind on my scavenger hunt. The bartenders who put these recipes together and made the drinks in front of judges would be happy to know we still think about them. I found the recipes in all sorts of places: souvenir cups, competition program books, cocktail books, newspaper clippings, websites, and more.

As you peel through these recipes, keep in mind that most of these drinks were created for cocktail competitions. Several of those competitions had some strict guidelines to follow, thus putting some constraints on creativity. As an example, the rules for the 1984 USBG Florida Chapter Cocktail Competition dictated that the drink needed to be an exotic drink containing any style of Pampero rum. As a result, you will find six drinks that are fairly similar to each other, with Pampero, pineapple juice, and a few other ingredients to balance out the drink. This doesn't mean there is not a lot of variety in this collection. Also, some of the names of these drinks reflect the customs and social conventions of the times. As an example: the *Hooker of 76* (P. 099).

As I read through these recipes, I noticed some glaring trends. From the late 1950s through the early 1980s, Falernum was used a lot. Galliano was even more popular; it can be found in several competition cocktails from the early 1950s to the turn of the century. And how about *crème de banane*? It, too, held strong for a fifty-year span beginning in the early 1950s. Frothee, the liquid cocktail foamer was the king of the 1970s. A few dashes were added to just about every cocktail of that decade.

I have so many questions I would have loved to ask their creators; I would ask Edward "Ed" Nordsiek why he has two cocktails that are 22 years apart from each other with identical names (Ed's Baby)(P. 091) and completely different ingredients? I would ask "Popo" Galsini why he chose the name *Saturn #2* (P. 121) for his 1968 cocktail that has no similarities with his *Saturn* cocktail (P. 121) from the year before? I would also ask him why he thinks his 1965 *Ponce De Lion* cocktail (P. 115) never became as popular as the Saturn cocktail despite the similarities and the fact that it came two years before *Saturn*? I am curious if John Rettino, who submitted a *Rum Runner* cocktail (P. 119) as a recipe in 1969, was aware that there was a popular drink with the same name (and endless variations) created nearly 20 years earlier. I would ask about portions, as a few drinks here add up to one and a half ounces (45 mL) of liquid and are served in regular glasses, so then what goes in the rest of the glass?

Only a handful of these cocktails ever became popular, but I highly recommend you spend some time checking them out, as you can find a few drinks you might like to riff on, just like the six contributors to this book did.

Some drinks were listed with recipes that resulted in a cloyingly sweet cocktail; in that case, I recommend using them as guidelines and adjusting to your liking.

A Blizzard

1 ounce / 30 mL orange vodka
1 ounce / 30 mL peach liqueur
½ ounce / 15 mL watermelon liqueur
Top with lemon-lime soda

Build over ice in a tall glass

— LYLE H. GORDON, USBG COCKTAIL COMPETITION, 1999

A Lulu

1 ounce / 30 mL light rum
½ ounce / 15 mL crème de noyaux
¼ ounce / 7 ½ mL Galliano liqueur
1 ounce / 30 mL orange juice
½ ounces / 15 mL passion fruit nectar

Shake and strain into a chilled tulip glass

— WILLIAM BROWN, CBG COCKTAIL COMPETITION, 1965

A Touch of Coral

1 ounce / 30 mL vodka
¾ ounce / 22 ½ mL Tuaca liqueur
¾ ounce / 22 ½ mL Tia Maria
½ ounce / 15 mL fresh orange juice
Dash of grenadine

Shake and strain into a coupe

— SAMUEL J. CHARD, CBG COCKTAIL COMPETITION, 1970

A Touch of Glass

1 ounce / 30 mL vodka
½ ounce / 15 mL Grand Marnier
½ ounce / 15 mL blue curaçao
1 ounce / 30 mL heavy cream
Dash of orange flower water

Shake and strain into a coupe

— JOHN R. BALTAZAR, USBG COCKTAIL COMPETITION, 1974

A Touch of Jade

1 ounce / 30 mL melon liqueur
½ ounce / 15 mL blue curaçao
½ ounce / 15 mL Mandarine Napoleon
½ ounce / 15 mL crème de banane
Top with ginger ale

Build over ice in a tall glass

— ROBERT G. IVERSON, USBG COCKTAIL COMPETITION, 1999

Adam's Mistake

1¼ ounces / 7½ mL brandy
¾ ounce / 22½ mL crème de cassis
1½ ounces / 15 mL lemon juice
¼ ounce / 7½ mL simple syrup
Dash of Frothee

Shake and strain over fresh ice into a tall glass

— PATRICK J. STAMBAUGH, CBG COCKTAIL COMPETITION, 1971

Anna's Delight

1½ ounces / 45 mL Cognac
½ ounce / 15 mL Casanova liqueur
½ ounce / 15 mL grenadine
½ ounce / 15 mL orange juice
½ ounce / 15 mL pineapple juice

Shake and strain into a coupe

— PHIL MARBACH, CBG COCKTAIL COMPETITION, 1965

Aloha

1 ounce / 30mL Puerto Rican light rum
½ ounce / 15mL Galliano liqueur
½ ounce / 15mL orange curaçao
1 ounce / 30mL lemon sour
½ ounce / 15mL piña colada mix
juice of ½ lime

Shake and strain over fresh ice into a tall glass

— HOWARD LEUNG, CBG COCKTAIL COMPETITION, 1970

Ambassador 76

1 ounce / 30 mL vodka
½ ounce / 15 mL sloe gin
½ ounce / 15 mL orange juice
½ ounce / 15 mL pineapple juice

Shake and strain into a coupe

— JAMES RYCHLY, USBG COCKTAIL COMPETITION, 1976

Angie's Cocktail

1½ ounces / 15 mL white rum
½ ounce / 15 mL Galliano liqueur
1¾ ounces / 22½ mL pineapple juice
¼ ounce / 7½ mL grenadine syrup

Shake and strain into a coupe

— RICHARD POUNCE, USBG COCKTAIL COMPETITION, 1972

Apollo

1 ounce / 30 mL applejack
¼ ounce / 7½ mL crème de banane
¼ ounce / 7½ mL grenadine
1 ounce / 30 mL lime juice

Shake and strain into a coupe

— WILLIAM MESSMER, CBG COCKTAIL COMPETITION, 1969

Apollo #2

1 ounce / 30 mL Puerto Rican light rum
¼ ounce / 7½ mL triple sec
¼ ounce / 7½ mL grenadine
¼ ounce / 7½ mL orange juice
¼ ounce / 7½ mL lemon juice

Shake and strain into a coupe

— ROBERT "BOB" WATSON, CBG COCKTAIL COMPETITION, 1970

Apple Annie

1 ounce / 30 mL vodka
¼ ounce / 7½ mL Galliano liqueur
¼ ounce / 7½ mL Grand Marnier
¼ ounce / 7½ mL lime juice
1 ounce / 30 mL apple juice

Build over ice in a tall glass

— PHILIP A. CORMIER, USBG COCKTAIL COMPETITION, 1970

Ariana's Dream

1 ounce / 30 mL white crème de cocoa
1 ounce / 30 mL Alizé Red Passion
½ ounce / 15 mL white rum
3 ounces / 90 mL orange juice

Blend with ice and serve in a tall glass

— FRUCTUOSO PRADO, USBG COCKTAIL COMPETITION, 1999

A-Ri-Rang

1 ounce / 30 mL vodka
½ ounce / 15 mL light rum
¼ ounce / 7½ mL white crème de cacao
2½ ounces / 75 mL orange juice
¼ ounce / 15 mL grenadine

Shake and strain over fresh ice into a tall glass

— SONG JUN YOON, USBG NATIONAL COCKTAIL COMPETITION, 1974

Arrowhead

1½ ounces / 45 mL vodka
½ ounce / 15 mL crème de noyaux
½ ounce / 15 mL cream of coconut
½ ounce / 15 mL pineapple juice

Shake and strain into a coupe

— JACK MCLAUGHLIN, USBG COCKTAIL COMPETITION, 1973

Astor Place

1 ounce / 30 mL orange vodka
½ ounce / 15 mL melon liqueur
½ ounce / 15 mL crème de banane
¾ ounce / 22½ mL sweet & sour

Shake and strain into a coupe

— JOHN W. CHOP, USBG BEFORE DINNER COCKTAIL COMPETITION, 1997

Auburn

1 ounce / 30 mL vodka
½ ounce / 15 mL crème de cassis
½ ounce / 15 mL Galliano liqueur
½ ounce / 15 mL orange juice

Shake and strain into a coupe

— KURT BEHRINGER, CBG COCKTAIL COMPETITION, 1966

Babylon Red

1 ounce / 30 mL vodka
¼ ounce / 7½ mL Grand Marnier
¼ ounce / 7½ mL Soranzo lemon liqueur
1½ ounces / 45 mL cranberry juice

Shake and strain into a coupe

— WILLIE LEE, USBG BEFORE DINNER COCKTAIL COMPETITION, 1997

Balkan Beauty

1¼ ounces / 40 mL vodka
½ ounce / 15 mL white crème de cacao
¼ ounce / 7½ mL crème de banane
¼ ounce / 7½ mL rock candy syrup
1 ounce / 30 mL lemon juice

Shake and strain into a coupe

— GARNET H. LONG, CBG COCKTAIL COMPETITION, 1968

Bambino

1 ounce / 30 mL brandy
¼ ounce / 7½ mL Myers's Original Rum Cream
¼ ounce / 7½ mL peppermint liqueur

Stir over ice in a beaker and strain into a coupe
Garnish with a cocktail cherry

— ALLAN NGAMINE, USBG HAWAII CHAPTER BEFORE DINNER COCKTAIL COMPETITION, 1983

Banana Bliss

1½ ounces / 45 mL VSOP Cognac
½ ounce / 15 mL crème de banane

Stir over ice in a beaker and strain into a coupe
Garnish with an orange peel

— EGIDIO "ANGUS" ANGEROSA FOUNDER OF THE UKBG–USA CHAPTER, 1930S

Banana Breeze

1½ ounces / 45 mL brandy
¼ ounce / 7½ mL apricot brandy
¾ ounce / 22½ mL crème de banane
1½ ounces / 45 mL orange juice
½ ounce / 15 mL lemon sour
3 dashes of Frothee

Shake and strain over fresh ice into a tall glass

— JOSE C. RUISECO, CBG COCKTAIL COMPETITION, 1970

Bandido

1 ounce / 30 mL tequila
½ ounce / 15 mL lime juice
¼ ounce / 7½ mL triple sec
Dash of grenadine
Dash of Frothee

Blend with ice and pour into a coupe

— CHARLES J. CHOP, USBG BEFORE DINNER COCKTAIL COMPETITION, 1997

Bavarian Mint

1 ounce / 30 mL white crème de menthe
1 ounce / 30 mL coffee liqueur
1 ounce / 30 mL heavy cream

Shake and strain into a coupe

— DONALD W. ALDRICH, USBG COCKTAIL COMPETITION, 1972

Beach Music

1½ ounces / 45 mL vodka
½ ounce / 15 mL peach liqueur
½ ounce / 15 mL lemon liqueur
½ ounce / 15 mL cranberry juice

Stir over ice in a beaker and strain into a coupe

— FRED D. IRETON, USBG BEFORE DINNER COCKTAIL COMPETITION, 1997

Belinda

1 ounce / 30 mL vodka
½ ounce / 15 mL orange curaçao
½ ounce / 15 mL apricot brandy
¼ ounce / 7½ mL grenadine
3 ounces / 90 mL orange juice

Blend with ice and serve in a tall glass
Garnish with a slice of pineapple, a cocktail cherry, and orchid

— ROBERT ACOBA, USBG HAWAII CHAPTER LONG DRINK COCKTAIL COMPETITION, 1983

Bernice

2 ounces / 60 mL vodka
1 ounce / 30 mL Galliano liqueur
Juice of ½ lime - drop hull
Dash of simple syrup
3 drops Pernod

Shake with cracked ice and strain into a coupe

— CHARLES BERNER, UKBG–USA WEST COAST COCKTAIL COMPETITION, 1950

Best Year

2¼ ounces / 70 mL vodka
2 ounces / 60 mL pineapple juice
¾ ounce / 22½ mL Licor 43
¾ ounce / 22½ mL blue curaçao
½ ounce / 15 mL lime cordial
Dash of simple syrup

Blend at high speed until smooth; pour into a tulip glass; fill with crushed ice; garnish with a pineapple spear picked to a cocktail cherry and a sprig of mint

— VALERIO "BOBBY" BATUGO, USBG COCKTAIL COMPETITION, 1974

Betty Dighton's Mint

2 ounces / 60 mL lemon flavored gin
½ ounce / 15 mL Campari
¾ ounce / 22½ mL orange juice
1 mint leaf

Shake and strain into a coupe

— EGIDIO "ANGUS" ANGEROSA — FOUNDER OF THE UKBG–USA CHAPTER, 1930S

Bichie Wichie

1¼ ounces / 37½ mL amber rum
½ ounce / 15 mL peach brandy
½ ounce / 15 mL crème de banane
1 ounce / 30 mL orange juice
½ ounce / 15 mL sweet & sour

Shake and strain over fresh ice into a tall glass

– AL YCOY, USBG NATIONAL COCKTAIL COMPETITION, 1974

Big Daddy

1 ounce / 30 mL brandy
½ ounce / 15 mL crème de banane
½ ounce / 15 mL white crème de cacao
1 ounce / 30 mL heavy cream

Shake and strain into a coupe

– PAUL CORNUKE, JR., USBG COCKTAIL COMPETITION, 1973

Big Mammo

1 ounce / 30 mL añejo rum
½ ounce / 15 mL orange curaçao
1 ounce / 30 mL pineapple juice
1 ounce / 30 mL sweet & sour
float of grenadine

Shake and strain over fresh ice into a tall glass

– CHARLES J. CHOP, USBG COCKTAIL COMPETITION, 1999

Binnacle

1¼ ounce / 40 mL Puerto Rican añejo rum
¼ ounce / 7½ mL Galliano liqueur
½ ounce / 15 mL passion fruit nectar
½ ounce / 15 mL lemon juice
3 dashes of Frothee

Shake and strain over fresh ice into a rocks glass

– SMITH LOWTHER, CBG COCKTAIL COMPETITION, 1968

Blue Bird

1½ ounces / 45 mL vodka
½ ounce / 15 mL Cointreau
½ ounce / 15 mL lemon juice
3 dashes of maraschino liqueur
3 dashes of blue extract

Shake and strain into a coupe

– WILLIAM "BILL" TARLING, FOUNDER OF THE UKBG, 1930S

Blue Bird #2

1½ ounces / 45 mL Pampero rum
½ ounce / 15 mL Licor 43
½ ounce / 15 mL sweet & sour

Shake and strain into coupe

– CARMEN FERRER, USBG FLORIDA BARTENDERS' GUILD COMPETITION, 1981

Blue Cobra

1 ounce / 30 mL vodka
½ ounce / 15 mL blue curaçao
½ ounce / 15 mL orgeat syrup
1½ ounces / 45 mL apple juice
1½ ounces / 45 mL coconut juice

Shake and strain over fresh ice into a tall glass

— PAUL CORNUKE JR., USBG NATIONAL COCKTAIL COMPETITION, 1974

Blue Finn

1¼ ounces / 37½ mL light rum
½ ounce / 15 mL blue curaçao
¼ ounce / 7½ mL orange juice
¼ ounce / 7½ mL pineapple juice

Shake and strain over fresh ice into a tall glass

— TED GENTRY, USBG NATIONAL COCKTAIL COMPETITION, 1974

Blue Gardenia

1 ounce / 30 mL Puerto Rican rum
½ ounce / 15 mL blue curaçao
¼ ounce / 7½ mL maraschino liqueur
¼ ounce / 7½ mL Parfait Amour liqueur
½ ounce / 15 mL heavy cream

Shake and strain into a coupe

— JOE "POPO" GALSINI, IBA COCKTAIL COMPETITION IN BERNE, SWITZERLAND, 1954

Blue Heaven

1 ounce / 30 mL Galliano liqueur
½ ounce / 15 mL blue curaçao
1 ounce / 30 mL sweet & sour
½ ounce / 15 mL pineapple juice

Shake and strain into a coupe

— LUKE QUAN, USBG COCKTAIL COMPETITION, 1972

Blue Horizon

1 ounce / 30 mL vodka
½ ounce / 15 mL blue curaçao
½ ounce / 15 mL orgeat syrup
1 ounce / 30 mL lemon juice

Shake and strain into a coupe

— ROBERT CALO, USBG COCKTAIL COMPETITION, 1976

Blue Lagoon

1 ounce / 30 mL vodka
½ ounce / 15 mL blue curaçao
½ ounce / 15 mL pineapple juice
½ ounce / 15 mL orange juice

Shake and strain into a coupe

— ROBERT G. IVERSON, USBG BEFORE DINNER COCKTAIL COMPETITION, 1997

Blue Max

1 ounce / 30 mL vodka
¼ ounce / 7½ mL Rock & Rye
½ ounce / 15 mL blue curaçao
½ ounce / 15 mL heavy cream
Dash of rock candy syrup

Shake and strain into a coupe

— MAX E. LYNCH, USBG COCKTAIL COMPETITION, 1974

Boob Ala

1¾ ounces / 55½ mL blanco tequila
1 ounce / 30 mL cranberry juice
½ ounce / 15 mL cream of coconut
¼ ounce / 7½ mL lime juice
Dash of Frothee

Shake and strain into a coupe

— GEORGE BENDINELLI, USBG COCKTAIL COMPETITION, 1976

Boom Boom

1 ounce / 30 mL añejo rum
¼ ounce / 7½ mL Licor 43
¼ ounce / 7½ mL crème de noyaux
1 ounce / 30 mL Sweet & sour
Dash of Frothee

Shake and strain into a coupe

— VIRGEL H. JONES, USBG COCKTAIL COMPETITION, 1976

Boomerang

1 ounce / 30 mL vodka
¼ ounce / 7½ mL Damiana liqueur
¼ ounce / 7½ mL triple sec
Dash of passion fruit nectar
twist of orange peel

Shake and strain over fresh ice into a rocks glass

— HANK WIRSTUK, CBG COCKTAIL COMPETITION, 1970

Bumble Bee

1 ounce / 30 mL gin
¼ ounce / 7½ mL crème de noyaux
1¼ ounces / 40 mL orange juice
Dash of rock candy syrup
Dash of Frothee
twist of orange peel

Shake and strain into a coupe

— GEORGE C. SPERDAKOS, USBG COCKTAIL COMPETITION, 1973

Cable Car

1½ ounces / 45 mL spiced rum
¾ ounce / 22½ mL orange curaçao
1½ ounces / 45 mL lemon sour

Shake, strain into a cinnamon-sugar rimmed cocktail glass
Garnish with an orange twist

— TONY ABOU-GANIM, HARRY DENTON'S STARLIGHT ROOM IN SAN FRANCISCO, 1996

Cabo Azul

½ ounce / 15 mL blue curaçao
1 ounce / 30 mL blanco tequila
2 ounces / 60 mL sweet & sour
1 ounce / 30 mL strawberry-kiwi liqueur

Build over ice in a tall glass

— DAN O'SHEA, USBG COCKTAIL COMPETITION, 1999

Canyon

1 ounce / 30 mL blanco tequila
½ ounce / 15 mL orange curacao
½ ounce / 15 mL grenadine
1 ounce / 30 mL orange juice
Dash of Frothee

Shake and strain into a coupe

— THOMAS MALTA, USBG COCKTAIL COMPETITION, 1976

Carmenita

1 ounce / 30 mL tequila
½ ounce / 15 mL apricot liqueur
¼ ounce / 7½ mL orange curaçao
¼ ounce / 7½ mL orgeat syrup
2 ounces / 60 mL orange juice

Shake and strain over fresh ice into a rocks glass

— EDWARD F. NORDSIEK, CBG COCKTAIL COMPETITION, 1969

Cecil's Dream

1 ounce / 30 mL rum
½ ounce / 15 mL Midori
½ ounce / 15 mL crème de cacao
1 ounce / 30 mL pineapple juice
Dash of simple syrup

Shake and strain into a coupe

— CESAR SANDOVAL, USBG BEFORE DINNER COCKTAIL COMPETITION, 1997

Ceiling Zero

1 ounce / 30 mL brandy
½ ounce / 15 mL orange curaçao
½ ounce / 15 mL crème de noyaux
1 ounce / 30 mL lemon sour

Shake and strain into a coupe

— CARL SWANSON, USBG COCKTAIL COMPETITION, 1972

C'est Si Bon

¾ ounce / 22½ mL amaretto
½ ounce / 15 mL Yukon Jack
¾ ounce / 22½ mL pineapple juice
Dash of orgeat syrup

Shake and strain into a coupe

— EARL TAKASAKI, USBG DRINK COMPETITION, 1983

Chococo Joe

1 ounce / 30 mL Puerto Rican añejo rum
½ ounce / 15 mL Chococo
¼ ounce / 7½ mL crème de banane
1¼ ounces / 40 mL heavy cream

Shake and strain into a coupe

— JOSEPH C. MEANEY, JR., USBG COCKTAIL COMPETITION, 1974

Chocolate Egg Crème

1 ounce / 30 mL chocolate liqueur
1 ounce / 30 mL vodka
2 ounces / 60 mL heavy cream
Soda water to fill

Chocolate syrup on rim of glass; shake first 3 ingredients, pour into chocolate rimmed glass. Fill with extra ice and soda and stir
Garnish with chocolate chips and miniature candy bars

— NAOMI FILBURN, USBG COCKTAIL COMPETITION, 1999

Chocolate Island

1¼ ounces / 40 mL chocolate liqueur
¼ ounce / 7½ mL coffee liqueur
¼ ounce / 7½ mL brandy
1¼ ounces / 40 mL heavy cream

Shake and strain into a coupe

— JOSEPH C. MEANEY, JR., USBG COCKTAIL COMPETITION, 1972

Chop Nut

1 ounce / 30 mL vodka
½ ounce / 15 mL crème de banane
½ ounce / 15 mL coconut juice
1 ounce / 30 mL orange juice
half egg whites

Shake and strain into a coupe

— JOHN W. CHOP, USBG COCKTAIL COMPETITION, 1977

Coconut Breeze

1½ ounces / 45 mL Jamaican rum
¼ ounce / 7½ mL pineapple juice
¼ ounce / 7½ mL coconut milk
Dash of orgeat syrup
Dash of maraschino syrup

Shake and strain into a coupe

— JOHN A. RETTINO, USBG COCKTAIL COMPETITION, 1976

Club House

1 ounce / 30 mL Puerto Rican rum
½ ounce / 15 mL Cherry Heering
½ ounce / 15 mL orgeat syrup
1 ounce / 30 mL orange juice

Shake and strain over fresh ice into a rocks glass

— AL CARRILLO, CBG COCKTAIL COMPETITION, 1976

Coca-Cooler

1 ounce / 30 mL coffee liqueur
½ ounce / 15 mL silver rum
½ ounce / 15 mL crème coconut syrup
2 ounces / 60 mL heavy cream

Shake and strain over fresh ice into a tall glass

— ROBERT WEALL, USBG HAWAII CHAPTER LONG DRINK COCKTAIL COMPETITION, 1983

Cocaretto

1¼ ounces / 40 mL vodka
½ ounce / 15 mL amaretto
¼ ounce / 7½ mL maraschino liqueur
1½ ounces / 45 mL Coca Cola
1½ ounces / 45 mL club soda

Build over ice in a tall glass
Garnish with a lemon wheel and serve with a long straw

— COLIN L. BULLARD, USBG HAWAII CHAPTER LONG DRINK COCKTAIL COMPETITION, 1983

Coco

1 ounce / 30 mL brandy
¾ ounce / 22½ mL crème de banane
1 ounce / 30 mL orange juice
½ ounce / 15 mL sweet & sour

Shake and strain into a coupe

— ANTONIO E. ANCONA, USBG COCKTAIL COMPETITION, 1976

Cocoa Frost

1 ounce / 30 mL Puerto Rican light rum
½ ounce / 15 mL crème de cocoa
½ ounce / 15 mL Galliano liqueur
1 ounce / 30 mL coconut juice
¼ ounce / 7½ mL rock candy syrup

Shake and strain into a coupe

— NICK BEEHLER, CBG COCKTAIL COMPETITION, 1965

Cognac Matinee

1 ounce / 30 mL cognac
¼ ounce / 7½ mL crème de banane
¼ ounce / 7½ mL Cointreau
½ ounce / 15 mL pineapple juice
¼ ounce / 7½ mL lime juice

Shake and strain over fresh ice into a tall glass

— ANTHONY V. CORDERO, CBG COCKTAIL COMPETITION, 1965

Cognac Perino

1 ounce / 30 mL VSOP cognac
½ ounce / 15 mL crème de banane
½ ounce / 15 mL passion fruit syrup
¼ ounce / 7½ mL Falernum
half egg whites
Squeeze ½ orange

Shake and strain over fresh ice into a tall glass

— ANTHONY V. CORDERO, USBG COCKTAIL COMPETITION, 1973

Cool Lagoon

1 ounce / 30 mL light rum
½ ounce / 15 mL green crème de menthe
½ ounce / 15 mL Liquore Sciarada
1 ounce / 30 mL pineapple juice

Shake and strain into a coupe

— DAVID L. SWORD, USBG COCKTAIL COMPETITION, 1976

Cool-One

1 ounce / 30 mL Puerto Rican rum
½ ounce / 15 mL triple sec
¼ ounce / 7½ mL cherry brandy
¼ ounce / 7½ mL orange juice
¼ ounce / 7½ mL pineapple juice

Shake and strain over fresh ice into a tall glass

— VIRGIL TROPEA, USBG NATIONAL COCKTAIL COMPETITION, 1974

Corpse Reviver #2

1 ounce / 30 mL gin
1 ounce / 30 mL Cointreau
1 ounce / 30 mL Lillet Blanc
1 ounce / 30 mL lemon juice
Dash of absinthe

Shake, strain into a coupe
Garnish with an orange peel

— HARRY CRADDOCK, 1ST PRESIDENT OF THE UKBG, 1920S

Cracklin' Rose

1¼ ounces / 40 mL Puerto Rican silver rum
½ ounce / 15 mL crème de banane
¾ ounce / 22½ mL passion fruit nectar
½ ounce / 15 mL pineapple juice
¼ ounce / 7½ mL lime juice

Shake and strain into a coupe

— VIRGEL H. JONES, USBG COCKTAIL COMPETITION, 1971

Crackling Rose

1¼ ounces / 40 mL light rum
½ ounce / 15 mL Passoã
¾ ounce / 22½ mL crème de noyaux
¾ ounce / 22½ mL sweetened lemon juice
½ ounce / 15 mL passion fruit nectar
half egg whites

Shake and strain into a coupe

— VIRGEL H. JONES, USBG COCKTAIL COMPETITION, 1971

Danish Fruit

1 ounce / 30 mL akvavit
½ ounce / 15 mL crème de banane
½ ounce / 15 mL peppermint schnapps
½ ounce / 15 mL orange juice

Shake and strain into a coupe

— KENNETH DECKER, CBG COCKTAIL COMPETITION, 1967

Derby Winner

¾ ounce / 22½ mL Tuaca liqueur
¾ ounce / 22½ mL Cointreau
1 ounce / 30 mL heavy cream

Shake and strain into a coupe

— THEODORE G. PARKER, USBG COCKTAIL COMPETITION, 1972

Desert Breeze

1½ ounces / 45 mL reposado tequila
½ ounce / 15 mL Midori liqueur
½ ounce / 15 mL Galliano liqueur
1½ ounces / 45 mL sweet & sour
3 ounces / 90 mL orange juice

Shake and strain over fresh ice into a tall glass

— ERVIN HARTUNG, SR., USBG COCKTAIL COMPETITION, 1999

Dimy's Baby

1 ounce / 30 mL vodka
¼ ounce / 7½ mL white crème de cacao
¼ ounce / 7½ mL crème de banane

Stir over ice in a beaker and strain into a coupe

— WILLIAM MESSMER, CBG COCKTAIL COMPETITION, 1967

Dolce Vita

1 ounce / 30 mL Jamaican rum
1 ounce / 30 mL pineapple juice
1½ ounces / 45 mL orange juice
Dash of orgeat syrup
Barspoon maraschino cherry syrup

Shake and strain over fresh ice into a tall glass

— JOHN A. RETTINO, USBG NATIONAL COCKTAIL COMPETITION, 1974

Don Calypso

1 ounce / 30 mL light rum
1 ounce / 30 mL apricot brandy
1 ounce / 30 mL pineapple juice

Shake and strain into a coupe

— DONALD W. ALDRICH, CBG COCKTAIL COMPETITION, 1969

Downtown

1 ounce / 30 mL gin
¾ ounce / 22½ mL melon liqueur
¼ ounce / 7½ mL Galliano liqueur
1 ounce / 30 mL yogurt mix
2 ounces / 60 mL pineapple juice
Dash of orgeat syrup

Blend with ice and serve in a tall glass
Garnish with a pineapple slice, fresh mint, an orchid, and a cocktail cherry

— RICK SUPNET, USBG HAWAII CHAPTER LONG DRINK COMPETITION, 1983

Dutch Kist

¾ ounce / 22½ mL Scotch whiskey
¼ ounce / 7½ mL Tiddy Liqueur
¼ ounce / 7½ mL Falernum
1 ounce / 30 mL orange juice

Shake and strain into a coupe

— LOUIS ESCOBEDO, CBG COCKTAIL COMPETITION, 1968

Ed's Baby

2 ounces / 60 mL light rum
Juice of ½ lime - drop hull
¼ ounce / 7½ mL crème de banane
¼ ounce / 7½ mL cherry liqueur
¼ ounce / 7½ mL orange curaçao

Shake with cracked ice and strain into a coupe

— EDWARD F. NORDSIEK, UKBG–USA WEST COAST COCKTAIL COMPETITION, 1952

Ed's Baby

1 ounce / 30 mL Puerto Rican rum
½ ounce / 15 mL orange curacao
¼ ounce / 7½ mL crème de banane
Dash of grenadine
juice of one large lime

Shake and strain over fresh ice into a tall glass

— EDWARD F. NORDSIEK, USBG NATIONAL COCKTAIL COMPETITION, 1974

El Boss

1½ ounces / 45 mL brandy
¾ ounce / 22½ mL melon liqueur
½ ounce / 15 mL banana liqueur
1½ ounces / 45 mL guava juice
1 ounce / 30 mL strawberry banana juice

Shake and strain over ice into a tall glass

— FELIPE GONZALEZ, USBG COCKTAIL COMPETITION, 1999

El Dante

1½ ounces / 45 mL brandy
½ ounce / 15 mL Grand Marnier
¼ ounce / 7½ mL anisette

Stir over ice in a beaker and strain into a coupe

— GEORGE BORELLA, USBG COCKTAIL COMPETITION, 1971

Entrepid

1 ounce / 30 mL gin
½ ounce / 15 mL Southern Comfort
¼ ounce / 7½ mL crème de noyaux
½ ounce / 15 mL orange juice
½ ounce / 15 mL lemon juice
¼ ounce / 7½ mL lime juice
Dash of orgeat syrup

Shake and strain over ice into a tall glass

— JOHN A. RETTINO, CBG COCKTAIL COMPETITION, 1970

Evening's Delight

1½ ounces / 45 mL Grand Marnier
1 ounce / 30 mL crème de banane
1 ounce / 30 mL pineapple Juice
1½ ounces / 45 mL heavy cream
Dash of Angostura bitters

Shake and strain into a chilled champagne glass

— NICK BEEHLER, UKBG–USA WEST COAST COCKTAIL COMPETITION, 1960

Fantastic

1 ounce / 30 mL brandy
½ ounce / 15 mL crème de noyaux
½ ounce / 15 mL crème de banane
½ ounce / 15 mL lemon juice
1 ounce / 30 mL orange juice
Dash of grenadine

Shake and strain into a coupe

— EDWARD D. O'BRIEN, USBG COCKTAIL COMPETITION, 1971

Finn And Fran

1½ ounce / 45 mL vodka
¾ ounce / 22½ mL Frangelico liqueur

Stir over ice in a beaker and strain into a coupe

— EUGENE COOLIK, USBG BEFORE DINNER COCKTAIL COMPETITION, 1997

First Blush

1 ounce / 30 mL citron vodka
1 ounce / 30 mL Charleston Follies
1 ounce / 30 mL orange juice
½ ounce / 15 mL cranberry juice
¼ ounce / 7½ mL Mele-Koi coconut snow

Shake the first four ingredients and strain over fresh ice, top with the coconut snow

— FRED IRETON, USBG COCKTAIL COMPETITION, 1999

Flamingo

1 ounce / 30 mL crème de banane
1 ounce / 30 mL white crème de cacao
2 ounces / 60 mL heavy cream
Dash of grenadine

Shake and strain into a coupe

— JOSE F. ANCONA, IBA WORLD COCKTAIL COMPETITION, 1993

Fran-Daddy

1 ounce / 30 mL Canadian whisky
½ ounce / 15 mL Tuaca liqueur
½ ounce / 15 mL crème de cassis
1 ounce / 30 mL sweet & sour

Shake and strain over ice into a tall glass

— EDWARD D. O'BRIEN, CBG COCKTAIL COMPETITION, 1969

French Kiss

1½ ounces / 45 mL rum
½ ounce / 15 mL crème de banane
½ ounce / 15 mL melon liqueur
2 ounces / 60 mL banana pineapple nectar
Top with lemon-lime soda

Shake the first four ingredients and strain into a tall glass over fresh ice, top with lemon-lime soda

— ALBERT J. REPETTY, USBG COCKTAIL COMPETITION, 1999

Frosty Dawn

2 ounces / 60 mL light rum
½ ounce / 15 mL maraschino liqueur
½ ounce / 15 mL Falernum
2 ounces / 60 mL orange juice

Shake with cracked ice and strain into a coupe

— ALBERT CARILLO, UKBG–USA WEST COAST COCKTAIL COMPETITION, 1960

Frosty Emerald

1½ ounces / 45 mL Midori liqueur
1 ounce / 30 mL wilderberry schnapps
½ ounce / 15 mL sweet & sour
Splash of lemon-lime soda
Top with club soda
Garnish, lime wedge and wheel and cocktail cherry/orange slice (Optional)

Build over ice in a tall glass

— PHIL KIRROS, USBG COCKTAIL COMPETITION, 1999

Funky Monkey

1½ ounces / 45 mL white rum
½ ounce / 15 mL crème de banane
¼ ounce / 7½ mL blue curaçao
1 ounce / 30 mL pineapple juice

Shake and strain into a coupe

— WILLIAM MCKEON, USBG COCKTAIL COMPETITION, 1976

Geine

1 ounce / 30 mL vodka
1 ounce / 30 mL Cointreau
½ ounce / 15 mL apricot brandy
½ ounce / 15 mL orange juice
juice of ½ Lime
2 dashes of grenadine

Shake and strain over ice into a tall glass

— DANNY JONES, CBG COCKTAIL COMPETITION, 1970

Gemini 13

1¼ ounces / 40 mL Puerto Rican silver rum
¾ ounce / 22½ mL crème de noyaux
½ ounce / 15 mL pineapple juice
½ ounce / 15 mL orange juice
¼ ounce / 7½ mL lime juice
2 dashes of Pernod

Shake and strain over fresh ice into a tall glass

— JESS MAGRO, CBG COCKTAIL COMPETITION, 1970

Gigi

1 ounce / 30 mL Puerto Rican light rum
½ ounce / 15 mL crème de noyaux
1 ounce / 30 mL orange juice
½ ounce / 15 mL lemon sour

Shake and strain into a coupe

— **DAVID STOCKER, USBG COCKTAIL COMPETITION 1973**

Gindori

1½ ounces / 45 mL gin
1 ounce / 30 mL Midori liqueur
1½ ounces / 45 mL pineapple juice

Blend with ice and pour into coupe

— **ARTURO A. PEINADO, USBG BEFORE DINNER COCKTAIL COMPETITION, 1997**

Glide'er Cocktail

1½ ounces / 45 mL tequila
¼ ounce / 7 ½ mL curaçao
½ ounce / 15 mL crème de noyaux
½ ounce / 15 mL lemon sour
½ ounce / 15 mL orange juice

Shake and strain over fresh ice into a tall glass

— **CARL SWANSON, USBG COCKTAIL COMPETITION, 1971**

Gold Swan

1 ounce / 30 mL vodka
½ ounce / 15 mL Galliano liqueur
1 ounce / 30 mL pineapple juice
½ ounce / 15 mL coconut juice
Dash of orgeat syrup

Shake and strain into a coupe

— **PAUL CORNUKE, JR., USBG COCKTAIL COMPETITION, 1976**

Golden Aggie

1 ounce / 30 mL vodka
¾ ounce / 22½ mL Galliano liqueur
½ ounce / 15 mL orange juice
1 ounce / 30 mL coconut milk

Shake and strain into a coupe

— **ROBERT KOEN, CBG COCKTAIL COMPETITION, 1967**

Golden Amber

1½ ounces / 45 mL demerara rum
1 ounce / 30 mL orange juice
½ ounce / 15 mL pineapple juice
½ ounce / 15 mL orgeat syrup

Shake and strain into a coupe

— **LEROY CHARON, CBG COCKTAIL COMPETITION, 1962**

Golden Comet

2 ounces / 60 mL London dry gin
¼ ounce / 7½ mL orange curaçao
¼ ounce / 7½ mL lime juice
Dash of simple syrup

Shake and strain into a coupe

— PETER ZAMUTO, UKBG–USA WEST COAST COCKTAIL COMPETITION, 1955

Golden Dream

1 ounce / 30 mL Galliano liqueur
1 ounce / 30 mL Cointreau
1 ounce / 30 mL orange juice
½ ounce / 15 mL heavy cream
Traditionally served with no garnish

Shake and strain into a coupe

— LEROY CHARON, UKBG–USA WEST COAST COCKTAIL COMPETITION, 1959

Golden Perino

1 ounce / 30 mL Cognac
¼ ounce / 7½ mL Cointreau
¼ ounce / 7½ mL white crème de cacao
½ ounce / 15 mL pineapple juice
¼ ounce / 7½ mL lime juice

Shake and strain over fresh ice into a tall glass

— ANTHONY V. CORDERO, CBG COCKTAIL COMPETITION, 1970

Golden Perino #2

1¼ ounces / 40 mL Puerto Rican silver rum
¾ ounce / 22½ mL crème de noyaux
¾ ounce / 22½ mL sweet & sour
½ ounce / 15 mL passion fruit nectar
½ ounce / 15 mL Fassionola
2 dashes of Frothee

Shake and strain over fresh ice into a rocks glass

— ANTHONY V. CORDERO, USBG COCKTAIL COMPETITION, 1971

Golden Princess

1 ounce / 30 mL American whiskey
¼ ounce / 7½ mL crème de banane
¼ ounce / 7½ mL maraschino liqueur
1 ounce / 30 mL orange juice
½ ounce / 15 mL passion fruit nectar
Dash of Frothee

Shake and strain over fresh ice into a rocks glass

— RICHARD MASTROSIMONE, USBG COCKTAIL COMPETITION, 1971

Gold Snake

1 ounce / 30 mL citrus rum
1 ounce / 30 mL Alize liqueur
½ ounce / 15 mL orange-banana liqueur
2 ounces / 60 mL cranberry juice
1½ ounce / 45 mL pineapple juice

Build over ice in a tall glass

— ARMANDO RODRIGUEZ, USBG COCKTAIL COMPETITION, 1999

Golden Star

1 ounce / 30 mL vodka
½ ounce / 15 mL amaretto
¼ ounce / 7½ mL maraschino liqueur
½ ounce / 15 mL orange juice
Dash of Frothee

Shake and strain into a coupe

— HANK WIRSTUK, USBG COCKTAIL COMPETITION, 1976

Golden Tail

1½ ounces / 45 mL Puerto Rican light rum
½ ounce / 15 mL Falernum
¾ ounce / 22½ mL guava pineapple nectar
½ ounce / 15 mL lemon sour

Blend over crushed ice and pour into a tulip glass

— JOSE C. YATCO, USBG COCKTAIL COMPETITION, 1971

Golden Touch

1 ounce / 30 mL silver rum
½ ounce / 15 mL white crème de cacao
1 ounce / 30 mL orange juice
½ ounce / 15 mL orgeat syrup

Shake and strain into a coupe

— WILLIAM BALOG, USBG COCKTAIL COMPETITION, 1972

Golden Trader

1 ounce / 30 mL Puerto Rican rum
½ ounce / 15 mL triple sec
1 ounce / 30 mL orange juice
½ ounce / 15 mL lemon sour

Shake and strain into a coupe

— JOSE C. YATCO, CBG COCKTAIL COMPETITION, 1967

Golden Turtle

1 ounce / 30 mL vodka
1 ounce / 30 mL crème de banana
1 ounce / 30 mL coconut juice
½ ounce / 15 mL orange juice

Shake and strain into a coupe

— ROBERT KOEN, CBG COCKTAIL COMPETITION, 1965

Golden Wave

2 ounces / 60 mL Puerto Rican rum
½ ounce / 15 mL Falernum
½ ounce / 15 mL Cointreau
1 ounce / 30 mL unsweetened pineapple juice
¾ ounce / 22½ mL lemon juice

Blend over crushed ice and pour into a tulip glass
Garnish with a pineapple spear and an orchid

— JOSE C. YATCO, CBG COCKTAIL COMPETITION, 1969

Golden Wench

1 ounce / 30 mL akvavit
1 ounce / 30 mL Strega liqueur
1 ounce / 30 mL orange juice
Dash of orgeat syrup

Shake and strain into a coupe

– KENNETH DECKER, CBG COCKTAIL COMPETITION, 1965

Granada

1½ ounces / 45 mL tequila
¾ ounce / 22½ mL Damiana liqueur
1 ounce / 30 mL lemon juice
Dash of grenadine

Shake and strain into a coupe

– JOSE F. ANCONA, CBG COCKTAIL COMPETITION, 1970

Green Eyes

1 ounce / 30 mL añejo rum
¾ ounce / 22½ mL Midori liqueur
1½ ounces / 45 mL pineapple juice
½ ounce / 15 mL coconut cream
½ ounce / 15 mL lime juice

Blend with ice and serve in a rocks glass Garnish with a lemon wheel

– ALBERT J. REPETTY, USBG NATIONAL COMPETITION, 1983

Green Wave

1 ounce / 30 mL gin
¼ ounce / 7½ mL green crème de menthe
½ ounce / 15 mL lime juice
¼ ounce / 7½ mL Galliano liqueur

Shake and strain into a coupe

– LYLE H. GORDON, USBG COCKTAIL COMPETITION, 1973

Gypsy

¾ ounce / 22½ mL gin
¾ ounce / 22½ mL Galliano liqueur
½ ounce / 15 mL grenadine
¾ ounce / 22½ mL heavy cream
Dash of Frothee

Shake and strain into a coupe

– VALERIO "BOBBY" BATUGO, USBG COCKTAIL COMPETITION, 1973

Heaven

1 ounce / 30 mL light rum
1 ounce / 30 mL crème de noyaux
1 ounce / 30 mL sweet & sour
1 ounce / 30 mL orange juice
Dash of Frothee

Shake and strain over fresh ice into a tall glass

– DAVID STOCKER, USBG NATIONAL COCKTAIL COMPETITION, 1974

Hey Panco

1 ounce / 30 mL Puerto Rican light rum
½ ounce / 15 mL coffee liqueur
½ ounce / 15 mL heavy cream
Dash of cherry juice

Shake and strain into a coupe

– PHILLIP A. CORMIER, USBG COCKTAIL COMPETITION, 1972

Hi-Fi

1 ounce / 30 mL Puerto Rican rum
½ ounce / 15 mL Suntory Cherry Blossom
½ ounce / 15 mL Licor 43
3 ounces / 90 mL orange juice
1 ounce / 30 mL pineapple juice

Shake and strain over fresh ice into a tall glass

– NICK KITCHUPOLOS, USBG NATIONAL COCKTAIL COMPETITION, 1974

High Tide

1½ ounces / 45 mL brandy
½ ounce / 15 mL Cherry Marnier
½ ounce / 15 mL passion fruit nectar
½ ounce / 15 mL Sweet & sour
Dash of grenadine

Shake and strain into a coupe

– ALBERT J. REPETTY, CBG COCKTAIL COMPETITION, 1968

Hody's Misty

1 ounce / 30 mL Cognac
¼ ounce / 7½ mL orange curaçao
¼ ounce / 7½ mL Cointreau
¼ ounce / 7½ mL Falernum

Stir over ice in a beaker and strain into a coupe

– ALBERT CARRILLO, CBG COCKTAIL COMPETITION, 1965

Honey Bear

1½ ounces / 45 mL vodka
¾ ounce / 22½ mL crème de banane
½ ounce / 15 mL Kahlua

Shake and strain into a coupe

– WELLS WESCOTT, USBG COCKTAIL COMPETITION, 1979

Honey Berry

1 ounce / 30 mL Puerto Rican rum
½ ounce / 15 mL Singal-Lignell & Piispanen Mesimarja
¼ ounce / 7½ mL kirsch
½ ounce / 15 mL pineapple juice
½ ounce / 15 mL lemon juice
¼ ounce / 7½ mL rock candy syrup
Dash of orgeat syrup

Shake and strain over fresh ice into a tall glass

– NICK BEEHLER, CBG COCKTAIL COMPETITION, 1967

Honeymoon

2 ounces / 60 mL brandy
½ ounce / 15 mL Cointreau
½ ounce / 15 mL Falernum
1 ounce / 30 mL orange juice

Shake with cracked ice and strain into a coupe

— ALBERT CARILLO, UKBG–USA WEST COAST COCKTAIL COMPETITION, 1958

Hooker of 76

1 ounce / 30 mL vodka
¼ ounce / 7½ mL Sciarada liqueur
¼ ounce / 7½ mL Galliano liqueur
½ ounce / 15 mL lime juice
Dash of Frothee

Shake and strain into a coupe

— CLAIRE L. REED, USBG COCKTAIL COMPETITION, 1976

Hornet

1¼ ounces / 40 mL applejack brandy
½ ounce / 15 mL Galliano liqueur
Juice of ½ lemon
½ ounce / 15 mL rock candy syrup
½ ounce / 15 mL cranberry juice

Shake and strain into a coupe

— THOMAS MALTA, USBG COCKTAIL COMPETITION, 1971

Icy Sea

1½ ounces / 45 mL rum
½ ounce / 15 mL dry gin
½ ounce / 15 mL lemon sour
½ ounce / 30 mL grenadine
½ ounce / 15 mL pineapple juice

Shake with cracked ice and strain over fresh ice into a tall glass

— VALERIO "BOBBY" BATUGO, IBA I.C.C. COCKTAIL COMPETITION, 1973

Innocent Eyes

1 ounce / 30mL Hawaiian silver rum
¾ ounce / 22½ mL crème de noyaux
¾ ounce / 22 ½ mL amaretto
½ ounce / 15mL fresh lime juice
¾ ounce / 22 ½ mL fresh orange juice

Shake and strain over fresh ice into a tall glass
Garnish with a pineapple wedge, mint, and an orchid

— SAM K.Y. HO, USBG HAWAII CHAPTER LONG DRINK COMPETITION, 1983

International Spice

1½ ounces / 45 mL spiced brandy
½ ounce / 15 mL Cointreau
½ ounce / 15 mL amaretto

Stir over ice in a beaker and strain into a coupe

— ALBERT J. REPETTY, USBG BEFORE DINNER COCKTAIL COMPETITION, 1997

Irish Affair

¾ ounce / 22½ mL blended Irish whiskey
¾ ounce / 22½ mL Kahlua
¼ ounce / 7½ mL orgeat syrup
1 ¼ ounces / 40 mL heavy cream
Dash of Frothee

Shake and strain into a coupe

— JOSE F. ANCONA, USBG COCKTAIL COMPETITION, 1973

Irish Greek

1 ounce / mL blended Irish whiskey
¾ ounce / 22½ mL green crème de menthe
1 ounce / 30 mL heavy cream
Dash of Ouzo
Dash of Frothee

Shake and strain into a coupe

— NICK KANELOS, USBG COCKTAIL COMPETITION, 1973

Irish Rover

1 ounce / 30 mL Irish whiskey
½ ounce / 15 mL cherry brandy
1 ounce / 30 mL lemon juice
¼ ounce / 7½ mL grenadine
Dash of Frothee

Shake and strain into a coupe

— RAYMUNDO B. MARTINEZ, USBG COCKTAIL COMPETITION, 1976

Irish Smash

1 ¼ ounces / 37½ mL blended Irish whiskey
¼ ounce / 7½ mL Vandermint liqueur
¼ tsp. bar sugar
4 ounces / 120 mL cold black coffee

Shake and strain over fresh ice into a tall glass

— W. JAKE OHLSEN, USBG NATIONAL COCKTAIL COMPETITION, 1974

Island Sunset

1 ounce / 30 mL Puerto Rican rum
¼ ounce / 7½ mL orange curaçao
¼ ounce / 7½ mL Galliano liqueur
1 ounce / 30 mL orange juice
½ ounce / 15 mL lemon juice

Shake and strain over fresh ice into a tall glass

— ALFREDO FONTANA, CBG COCKTAIL COMPETITION, 1968

Jealousy

1 ounce / 30 mL white rum
½ ounce / 15 mL Soranzo lemon liqueur
½ ounce / 15 mL melon liqueur
1 ounce / 30 mL sweet & sour
1 ounce / 30 mL orange juice

Shake and strain into a coupe

— VIRGEL H. JONES, USBG BEFORE DINNER COCKTAIL COMPETITION, 1997

Jewel's Delight

1 ounce / 30 mL vodka
½ ounce / 15 mL Grand Marnier
1½ ounces / 45 mL orange juice

Shake and strain into a coupe

— CHAMP CLARK, USBG COCKTAIL COMPETITION, 1976

Jojo Lou

1 ½ ounces / 45 mL applejack brandy
½ ounce / 15 mL crème de noyaux
½ ounce / 15 mL pineapple juice
½ ounce / 15 mL orange juice
Dash of grenadine
Dash of Frothee

Shake and strain into a coupe

— JOHN DUFF JR., USBG COCKTAIL COMPETITION, 1971

Jojo Lou The II

1 ½ ounces / 45 mL Puerto Rican silver rum
½ ounce / 15 mL crème de noyaux
½ ounce / 15 mL Galliano liqueur
1 ounce / 30 mL heavy cream
sprinkle of nutmeg

Shake and strain into a coupe

— JOHN T. DUFF JR., USBG COCKTAIL COMPETITION, 1972

Jose's Siesta

1 ounce / 30 mL gold tequila
¼ ounce / 7½ mL crème de noyaux
¼ ounce / 7½ mL orgeat syrup
4 ounces / 120 mL orange juice
1 ounce / 30 mL lime juice

Shake and strain over fresh ice into a tall glass

— RAY L. SWANSON, USBG NATIONAL COCKTAIL COMPETITION, 1974

Ka Va

1 ½ ounces / 45 mL apple brandy
½ ounces / 15 mL yellow Chartreuse
¾ ounces / 22½ mL pineapple juice
½ ounces / 15 mL orange juice

Shake and strain into a coupe

— ROBERT GORDON, CBG COCKTAIL COMPETITION, 1969

Kay's Kooler

1½ ounces / 45 mL vodka
½ ounce / 15 mL Galliano liqueur
½ ounce / 15 mL grenadine
½ ounce / 15 mL sweet & sour
½ ounce / 15 mL orange juice

Shake and strain over fresh ice into a tall glass

— EDWARD O'BRIEN, USBG NATIONAL COCKTAIL COMPETITION, 1974

Kentucky Sunset

1½ ounces / 45 mL Bourbon whiskey
½ ounce / 15 mL Strega
½ ounce / 15 mL anisette
Twist orange peel

Stir over ice in a beaker and strain into a coupe

— PABLO L. ACEVEDO, EARLY TIMES NATIONAL MIXED CONTEST, 1957

Kesha

1 ounce / 30 mL vodka
1 ounce / 30 mL Cointreau
½ ounce / 15 mL coconut milk
½ ounce / 15 mL heavy cream

Shake and strain into a coupe

— WILLIAM BRADFORD, USBG COCKTAIL COMPETITION, 1974

Kim

2 ounces / 60 mL brandy
½ ounce / 15 mL Triple Sec
1 ounce / 30 mL Galliano liqueur
½ ounce / 15 mL lemon juice

Shake and strain into a coupe

— JOHN DURLESSER, CBG COCKTAIL COMPETITION, 1973

King Edward

1 ounce / 30 mL dry gin
1 ounce / 30 mL Sciarada
1½ ounces / 45 mL sweet & sour
1 tsp. of coco syrup
Dash of Frothee

Shake and strain into a coupe

— EDWARD F. NORDSIEK, USBG COCKTAIL COMPETITION, 1976

Kool Banana

1 ounce / 30 mL crème de banane
¾ ounce / 22½ mL Triple Sec
¼ ounce / 7½ mL grenadine
1 ounce / 30 mL heavy cream
Dash of Frothee

Shake and strain into a coupe

— ALBERT J. REPETTY, USBG COCKTAIL COMPETITION, 1972

La Vita Doucke

1½ ounces / 45 mL coffee vodka
1 ounce / 30 mL lemon liqueur

Stir over ice in a beaker and strain into a coupe

— VIRGIL TROPEA, USBG BEFORE DINNER COCKTAIL COMPETITION, 1997

Ladies Pampero

1 ounce / 30 mL Pampero rum
½ ounce / 15 mL Aricoco
½ ounce / 15 mL Choco Clair
½ ounce / 15 mL heavy cream

Shake and strain into a coupe

— MAX DE LA FUENTE, USBG FLORIDA BARTENDERS' GUILD COMPETITION, 1981

Lancer

1½ ounces / 45 mL Puerto Rican light rum
¼ ounce / 7½ mL coconut juice

Stir over ice in a beaker and strain into a coupe

— GIL LEVY, CBG COCKTAIL COMPETITION, 1969

Latin Lace

1 ounce / 30 mL Mexican coffee liqueur
½ ounce / 15 mL Triple Sec
½ ounce / 15 mL orange juice
1 ounce / 30 mL heavy cream

Shake and strain into a coupe

— JERRY KEHL, USBG COCKTAIL COMPETITION, 1972

Leg Before Wicket

2 ounces / 60 mL London Dry gin
¼ ounce / 7½ mL Campari
½ ounce / 15 mL Dubonnet
¼ ounce / 7½ mL lime juice

Stir over ice in a beaker and strain into a coupe

— EGIDIO "ANGUS" ANGEROSA – FOUNDER OF THE UKBG–USA CHAPTER, 1930S

Lily

1 ounce / 30 mL Puerto Rican light rum
1 ounce / 30 mL Galliano liqueur
1 ounce / 30 mL orange juice
1 ounce / 30 mL passion fruit juice

Shake and strain into a coupe

— RICHARD POUNCE, CBG COCKTAIL COMPETITION, 1970

Linda Lou

1 ounce / 30 mL vodka
½ ounce / 15 mL Galliano liqueur
¼ ounce / 7½ mL Grand Marnier
1 ounce / 30 mL orange juice
Dash of Frothee

Shake and strain into a coupe

— WILLIAM PATRICK BRYAN, CBG COCKTAIL COMPETITION, 1969

Little Cooler

4 ounces / 120 mL Champagne
1 ounce / 30 mL VSOP Cognac
½ ounce / 15 mL Cherry Heering
Traditionally served with no garnish

Stir the first two ingredients and strain into a flute, top with Champagne

— **BRIAN F. REA – FOUNDER OF THE UKBG, USA EAST COAST CHAPTER, DINER'S CLUB COCKTAIL COMPETITION, 1958**

Long Beach Shake

1 ounce / 30 mL rum
1 ounce / 30 mL chocolate liqueur
½ ounce / 15 mL Irish cream
3 ounces / 90 mL heavy cream
Dash of grenadine

Shake and strain into a coupe

— **VINCENT CISNEROS, USBG COCKTAIL COMPETITION, 1999**

Lost Streaker

¾ ounce / 22½ mL brandy
¾ ounce / 22½ mL Galliano liqueur
¾ ounce / 22½ mL pineapple juice
¾ ounce / 22½ mL heavy cream
Dash of orange bitters

Shake and strain into a coupe

— **JOHN J. GILBERT, USBG COCKTAIL COMPETITION, 1974**

Louise

1 ounce / 30 mL brandy
½ ounce / 15 mL Cointreau
1¼ ounces / 40 mL orange juice
¼ ounce / 7½ mL grenadine

Shake and strain into a coupe

— **FERROL ARCHER, USBG COCKTAIL COMPETITION, 1974**

Lovely Lady

1¼ ounces / 7½ mL Puerto Rican rum
½ ounce / 15 mL orange curaçao
½ ounce / 15 mL pineapple juice
½ ounce / 15 mL cranberry juice

Shake and strain into a coupe

— **JESS MAGRO, CBG COCKTAIL COMPETITION, 1967**

Lovers' Kiss

¾ ounce / 22½ mL rum
¾ ounce / 22½ mL Licor 43
¼ ounce / 7½ mL piña colada mix
1¾ ounces / 52½ mL orange juice
Dash of grenadine

Shake and strain over fresh ice into a tall glass

— **JAIME BAJO, USBG NATIONAL LONG DRINK COMPETITION, 1983**

Lu

1 ounce / 30 mL brandy
¼ ounce / 7½ mL Galliano liqueur
¼ ounce / 7½ mL passion fruit nectar
½ ounce / 15 mL orange juice

Shake and strain into a coupe

– WILLIAM "BILL" BROWN, CBG COCKTAIL COMPETITION, 1967

Lu II

1 ounce / 30 mL brandy
¼ ounce / 7½ mL Galliano liqueur
¼ ounce / 7½ mL passion fruit nectar
½ ounce / 15 mL orange juice
¼ ounce / 7½ mL crème de noyaux

Shake and strain into a coupe

– WILLIAM "BILL" BROWN, CBG COCKTAIL COMPETITION, 1969

Lucky Concoction

1 ounce / 30 mL crème de banane
1 ounce / 30 mL brandy
½ ounce / 15 mL amaretto
1½ ounces / 45 mL orange juice
1 ounce / 30 mL pineapple juice

Build over ice in a tall glass

– JOSE RUISECO, USBG COCKTAIL COMPETITION, 1999

Luxury

1 ounce / 30 mL London dry gin
1 ounce / 30 mL Pimm's Cup No. 1
½ ounce / 15 mL sweet vermouth
¼ ounce / 7½ mL banana liqueur
½ ounce / 15 mL lime juice
¼ ounce / 7½ mL simple syrup
Dash of Angostura bitters

Shake with cracked ice and strain into a coupe

– WALTER SIMPSON, UKBG–USA WEST COAST COCKTAIL COMPETITION, 1951

Macarena

1½ ounces / 45 mL pineapple vodka
½ ounce / 15 mL Chambord liqueur
¼ ounce / 7½ mL sweet & sour
½ ounce / 15 mL orange juice
½ ounce / 15 mL cranberry juice

Shake and strain into a coupe

– FELIPE GONZALEZ, USBG BEFORE DINNER COCKTAIL COMPETITION, 1997

Magic Castle

1 ounce / 30 mL Tuaca liqueur
½ ounce / 15 mL chocolate liqueur
1½ ounces / 45 mL heavy cream

Shake and strain into a coupe

– JOHN E. BEECHLER, USBG COCKTAIL COMPETITION, 1972

Malibu Orchid

1 ¼ ounces / 40 mL Malibu rum
1 ounce / 30 mL cranberry juice
¾ ounce / 22 ½ mL pineapple juice
½ ounce / 15 mL orgeat syrup
¼ ounce / 7½ mL lime juice

Shake and strain over fresh ice into a tall glass

— **KELLY LIGHTNER, USBG COCKTAIL COMPETITION, 1985**

Malla

1¼ ounce / 37½ mL Puerto Rican light rum
¼ ounce / 7½ mL orgeat syrup
½ ounce / 15 mL pineapple juice
½ ounce / 15 mL lemon juice

Shake and strain into a coupe

— **ROBERT GORDON, CBG COCKTAIL COMPETITION, 1965**

Manzanita

1 ounce / 30 mL applejack brandy
½ ounce / 15 mL orange curaçao
½ ounce / 15 mL grenadine
1 ounce / 30 mL orange juice
1 ounce / 30 mL sweet & sour

Shake and strain over fresh ice into a tall glass

— **VINCENT GIULIANI, USBG NATIONAL COCKTAIL COMPETITION, 1974**

Maple Leaf

1¼ ounces / 40 mL Canadian whisky
½ ounce / 15 mL Galliano liqueur
¼ ounce / 7½ mL Cointreau
½ ounce / 15 mL passion fruit nectar
¼ ounce / 7½ mL lime juice
2 dashes of Frothee
Twist of orange peel

Shake and strain over fresh ice into a tall glass

— **OSCAR DE LA LIATA, USBG COCKTAIL COMPETITION, 1971**

Margarita (Durlessor's Way)

1¾ ounces / 50 mL gold tequila
¾ ounce / 22½ mL Cointreau
1 ounce / 30 mL lime juice

Shake and strain into a salt-rimmed coupe

— **JOHN DURLESSER, COFOUNDER OF THE USA–UKBG–WEST COAST CHAPTER, POPULARIZED THIS DRINK IN 1954.**

Martinee Cocktail

1 ounce / 30 mL Cognac
¼ ounce / 7½ mL crème de banane
¼ ounce / 7½ mL Cointreau
½ ounce / 15 mL pineapple juice
½ ounce / 15 mL lime juice

Shake and strain into a coupe

— **ANTHONY V. CORDERO, CBG COCKTAIL COMPETITION, 1967**

Mary Rose

1 ounce / 30 mL Puerto Rican light rum
½ ounce / 15 mL Cherry Heering
½ ounce / 15 mL white crème de cacao
1 ounce / 30 mL heavy cream

Shake and strain into a coupe

— ROBERT SULLIVAN, USBG COCKTAIL COMPETITION, 1974

Mellow Yellow

1½ ounces / 45 mL vodka
¾ ounce / 22½ mL Southern Comfort
½ ounce / 15 mL Galliano liqueur
¼ ounce / 7½ mL lime juice
Dash of Pernod

Stir over ice in a beaker and strain into a coupe

— SAMUEL CHARD, CBG COCKTAIL COMPETITION, 1968

Melonaire

1 ounce / 30 mL Midori liqueur
½ ounce / 15 mL crème de banane
½ ounce / 15 mL Triple Sec
1 ounce / 30 mL sweet & sour

Shake and strain into a coupe

— JOHN W. CHOP, USBG BEFORE DINNER DRINK COMPETITION, 1983

Melotini

½ ounce / 15 mL Midori liqueur
1 ounce / 30 mL extra dry vermouth
½ ounce / 15 mL pineapple juice
½ ounce / 15 mL lemon juice
Dash of Angostura

Stir over ice in a beaker and strain into a coupe

— DADYNSKI BOGDAN, USBG BEFORE DINNER COCKTAIL COMPETITION, 1997

Memmories (*aka* Memories)

1¼ ounces / 40 mL amaretto
1 ounce / 30 mL Irish cream
½ ounce / 15 mL blue curaçao
1 drop of lemon juice
Dash of Frothee

Shake and pour into a chilled tulip glass

— VALERIO "BOBBY" BATUGO, USBG COCKTAIL COMPETITION, 1973

Merry Jo

1¼ ounces / 40 mL Bourbon
½ ounce / 15 mL grenadine
¼ ounce / 7½ mL Pernod
¾ ounce / 22½ mL lemon juice

Shake and strain into a coupe

— LE ROY CHARON, CBG COCKTAIL COMPETITION, 1968

Merry K

2½ ounces / 75 mL Bourbon
½ ounce / 15 mL orange curaçao
Twist of orange peel

Stir over ice in a beaker and strain into a coupe

— THOMAS E STENGER, UKBG–USA WEST COAST COCKTAIL COMPETITION, 1956

Mexitalian

1 ounce / 30 mL vodka
½ ounce / 15 mL coffee liqueur
½ ounce / 15 mL Galliano liqueur

Shake and strain into a coupe

— OTTO EIGENMANN, USBG COCKTAIL COMPETITION, 1976

Midnight Express

1 ounce / 30 mL vodka
1 ounce / 30 mL Midori liqueur
½ ounce / 15 mL coconut liqueur
2 ounces / 60 mL pineapple juice
1 ounce / 30 mL cranberry juice

Build over ice in a tall glass

— BYRON NEVAREZ, USBG COCKTAIL COMPETITION, 1999

Midnight Sun

¾ ounce / 22½ mL crème de banane
¾ ounce / 22½ mL orange curaçao
½ ounce / 15 mL lemon sour
1 ounce / 30 mL heavy cream
Dash of Frothee

Shake and strain into a coupe

— JOHN W. CHOP, USBG COCKTAIL COMPETITIONS, 1972

Miss Marnie

1½ ounces / 45 mL brandy
½ ounce / 15 mL crème de banane
½ ounce / 15 mL cranberry apple juice
½ ounce / 15 mL orange juice
½ ounce / 15 mL lemon juice
Dash of grenadine

Shake and strain into a coupe

— JAMES "JIMMY" P. CAMPBELL, CBG COCKTAIL COMPETITION, 1969

Miss Marnie #2

1½ ounces / 45 mL brandy
1 ounce / 30 mL coconut-pineapple mix
½ ounce / 15 mL lemon juice
Dash of grenadine

Shake and strain into a coupe

— JAMES "JIMMY" P. CAMPBELL, CBG COCKTAIL COMPETITION, 1970

Miss Marnie #3

1 ounce / 30 mL brandy
½ ounce / 15 mL Vandermint liqueur
½ ounce / 15 mL cherry juice
1 ounce / 30 mL heavy cream
Dash of Frothee

Shake and strain into a coupe

— JAMES "JIMMY" P. CAMPBELL, USBG COCKTAIL COMPETITION, 1974

Misty

1 ounce / 30 mL gin
½ ounce / 15 mL Galliano liqueur
½ ounce / 15 mL Triple Sec
½ ounce / 15 mL lime juice sweetened

Shake and strain into a coupe

— LEONARD "LENNY" CASTEEL, CBG COCKTAIL COMPETITION, 1969

Misty

1 ounce / 30 mL gin
¾ ounce / 22½ mL peach curaçao
¾ ounce / 22½ mL Drambuie
½ ounce / 15 mL lemon juice

Shake and strain over fresh ice into a tall glass. Garnish with a lemon slice.

— JOSE MANZANO, USBG HAWAII CHAPTER BEFORE DINNER COCKTAIL COMPETITION, 1983

Misty Breeze

1 ounce / 30 mL white chocolate liqueur
½ ounce / 15 mL strawberry syrup
1 ounce / 30 mL raspberry schnapps
1 ounce / 30 mL heavy cream
splash of lime juice
half egg whites

Shake and strain into a coupe
Garnish with a whole strawberry

— FRED IRETON, USBG COCKTAIL COMPETITION, 1990

Misty Miss

1 ounce / 30 mL apricot brandy
¾ ounce / 22½ mL Strega liqueur
¾ ounce / 22½ mL heavy cream
¾ ounce / 22½ mL orange juice

Shake and strain into a coupe

— VIRGIL TROPEA, USBG COCKTAIL COMPETITION, 1972

Molly Brown

1 ounce / 30 mL Aalborg Akvavit
½ ounce / 15 mL orange curaçao
½ ounce / 5 mL lime cordial

Stir over ice in a beaker and strain into a coupe

— ALAN D. SPEAR, CBG COCKTAIL COMPETITION, 1965

Moonglow

1 ounce / 30 mL vodka
½ ounce / 15 mL Galliano liqueur
½ ounce / 15 mL Triple Sec
½ ounce / 15 mL lime juice

Shake and strain into a coupe

— JOHN W. CHOP, CBG COCKTAIL COMPETITION, 1968

Moonglow

¾ ounce / 22½ mL amaretto
1½ ounces / 45 mL dry blanc vermouth

Stir over ice in a beaker and strain into a coupe

— SEAN DUKERICH, USBG COCKTAIL COMPETITION, 1983

Morton's Delight

1 scoop vanilla ice cream
½ ounce / 15 mL amaretto
½ ounce / 15 mL Grand Marnier
½ ounce / 15 mL Kahlua
½ ounce / 15 mL orange juice

Blend with half scoop of ice and serve in a tall glass

— SHIRLEY MORTON, USBG NATIONAL LONG DRINK COMPETITION, 1983

MS

1 ounce / 30 mL vodka
½ ounce / 15 mL crème de banane
½ ounce / 15 mL crème de noyaux
1 ounce / 30 mL heavy cream
Dash of orgeat syrup
Dash of Frothee

Shake and strain into a coupe

— JOHN W. CHOP, USBG, 1974

Muddy Mango

1 ounce / 30 mL passion mango liqueur
1 ounce / 30 mL parfait amour
2½ ounces / 15 mL mango juice
Dash of grenadine
Top with lemon-lime soda

Build over ice in a tall glass

— JOSE F. ANCONA, USBG COCKTAIL COMPETITION, 1999

My Diane

1 ounce / 30 mL gin
½ ounce / 15 mL Galliano liqueur
½ ounce / 15 mL Grand Marnier
½ ounce / 15 mL orange juice
½ ounce / 15 mL coconut milk

Shake and strain over ice into a tall glass

— WILLIAM PATRICK BRYAN, CBG COCKTAIL COMPETITION, 1968

My Dream

¾ ounce / 22½ mL Galliano liqueur
¾ ounce / 22½ mL orange curaçao
¾ ounce / 22½ mL pineapple juice
¾ ounce / 22½ mL heavy cream
Twist of orange peel

Shake and strain into a coupe

— FRANCOIS MOUVET, USBG COCKTAIL COMPETITION, 1972

My Julie

1½ ounces / 45 mL vodka
¾ ounce / 22½ mL sweet vermouth
¼ ounce / 7½ mL heavy cream
½ ounce / 15 mL sweet & sour
Dash of grenadine

Shake and strain into a coupe

— FREDERICK A. BOYD, USBG COCKTAIL COMPETITION, 1974

Nancy's Fancy

1 ounce / 30 mL brandy
½ ounce / 15 mL Galliano liqueur
½ ounce / 15 mL orange curaçao
½ ounce / 15 mL lemon juice
½ ounce / 15 mL orange juice
2 dashes of orange flower water
2 dashes of grenadine

Shake and strain over fresh ice into a tall glass

— JAMES P MCCANN, CBG COCKTAIL COMPETITION, 1965

Natasha Princess

¾ ounce / 22½ mL orange vodka
¼ ounce / 7½ mL mango passion liqueur
½ ounce / 15 mL crème de banane
1½ ounces / 45 mL orange juice

Shake and strain into a coupe

— JOSE F. ANCONA, USBG BEFORE DINNER COCKTAIL COMPETITION, 1997

Night Cap

1½ ounce / 45 mL gin
½ ounce / 15 mL grenadine
½ ounce / 15 mL Falernum
1 ounce / 30 mL pineapple juice
1½ ounces / 45 mL orange juice

Shake and strain over fresh ice into a tall glass
Garnish with an orange wheel and a cocktail cherry

— TITO LEDDA, USBG HAWAII CHAPTER LONG DRINK COMPETITION, 1983

On The Green

1½ ounces / 45 mL vodka
¾ ounce / 22½ mL Galliano liqueur
¾ ounce / 22½ mL Midori liqueur

Stir over ice in a beaker and strain into a coupe

— AYOE NIELSEN, USBG BEFORE DINNER COCKTAIL COMPETITION, 1997

Orange Coast

1½ ounces / 45 mL white rum
1½ ounces / 45 mL Midori liqueur
1½ ounces / 45 mL pineapple juice
1½ ounces / 45 mL orange juice
Float ½ ounce / 15 mL grenadine

Blend with ice and serve in a tall glass

— JASON HULBERT, USBG COCKTAIL COMPETITION, 1999

Orange Glo

1 ounce / 30 mL Cognac
½ ounce / 15 mL orange curaçao
½ ounce / 15 mL Triple Sec
1 ounce / 30 mL orange juice
Orange twist

Shake and strain into a coupe

— ALFREDO FONTANA, BARTENDERS' GUILD (CBG) COCKTAIL COMPETITION, 1969

O'suzanna

1 ounce / 30 mL vodka
1 ounce / 30 mL crème de noyaux
2 ounces / 60 mL margarita mix
2 ounces / 60 mL orange juice

Shake with cracked ice and strain into a tall glass

— VIRGEL H. JONES, USBG NATIONAL LONG DRINK COMPETITION, 1999

Pagans Explosion

1 ounce / 30 mL tequila
½ ounce / 15 mL Licor 43
½ ounce / 15 mL cherry brandy
3 ounces / 120 mL orange juice
6 drops of grenadine

Shake and strain over fresh ice into a tall glass

— AL CONKLIN, USBG NATIONAL COCKTAIL COMPETITION, 1974

Pampero Dream

1 ounce / 30mL Pampero añejo rum
½ ounce / 15 mL blue curaçao
¼ ounce / 7½ mL Cointreau
2 ounces / 60 ml pineapple juice
Dash of lemon juice

Blend with ice and serve in a tall glass

— NORMANDO CAMPOS, USBG FLORIDA BARTENDERS' GUILD COMPETITION, 1981

Pandora

1 ounce / 30 mL brandy
½ ounce / 15 mL crème de noyaux
½ ounce / 15 mL Grand Marnier
1 ounce / 30 mL sweet & sour
Dash of Frothee
Dash of orange flower water

Shake and strain over fresh ice into a tall glass

— WILLIAM WEIDMAN, USBG COCKTAIL COMPETITION, 1973

Passion Ora

1¼ ounces / 40mL brandy
¾ ounce / 22 ½ mL Lochan Ora Whisky liqueur
½ ounce / 15 mL passion fruit nectar
Dash of Frothee
Oil expressed from the twist of orange peel

Shake and strain into a coupe

— OSCAR DE LA LIATA, USBG COCKTAIL COMPETITION, 1972

Patrician Cocktail

1 ounce / 30 mL Canadian whisky
½ ounce / 15 mL Grand Marnier
½ ounce / 15 mL Galliano liqueur
½ ounce / 15 mL orange juice

Shake and strain into a coupe

— EGIDIO "ANGUS" ANGEROSA, CBG COCKTAIL COMPETITION, 1965

Patti-Lu

1½ ounces / 45 mL gold rum
½ ounce / 15 mL crème de almond
¼ ounce / 7½ mL Roiano Liqueur
1 ounce / 30 mL orange juice
½ ounce / 15 mL passion fruit nectar

Shake and strain over fresh ice into a tall glass

— BILL BROWN, USBG NATIONAL COCKTAIL COMPETITION, 1974

Pazazz

1 ounce / 30 mL Puerto Rican silver rum
¾ ounce / 22½ mL Grand Marnier
½ ounce / 15 mL lime juice
½ ounce / 15 mL pineapple juice

Shake and strain into a coupe

— WILLIAM J. COLONA, USBG COCKTAIL COMPETITION, 1970

Peach Blossom

1¼ ounces / 7½ mL brandy
½ ounce / 15 mL peach brandy
1½ ounce / 15 mL orange juice
Dash of grenadine
Dash of Frothee

Shake and strain into a coupe

— AL YCOY, USBG COCKTAIL COMPETITION, 1972

Peach Fuzz

1 ounce / 30 mL gin
½ ounce / 15 mL peach brandy
1 ounce / 30 mL pineapple juice
½ ounce / 15 mL sweet & sour

Shake and strain into a coupe

— FRANK J. BOWMAN, USBG COCKTAIL COMPETITION, 1976

Perino Cup

1½ ounces / 45 mL light rum
¼ ounce / 7½ mL crème de banane
¼ ounce / 7½ mL Cointreau
¼ ounce / 7½ mL pineapple juice
½ ounce / 15mL lime juice
2 dashes of Peychaud's bitters

Shake and strain over fresh ice into a tall glass

– ANTHONY V. CORDERO, CBG COCKTAIL COMPETITION, 1969

Petake (aka Pikake)

2 ounce / 60 mL light rum
½ ounce / 15 mL Van der Hum
¼ ounce / 7½ mL Cointreau
Juice of half lime - drop hull
½ ounce / 15 mL pineapple juice
½ ounce / 15 mL papaya juice

Shake with cracked ice and strain into a coupe

– JOE "POPO" GALSINI, UKBG–USA WEST COAST COCKTAIL COMPETITION, 1953

Pink Banana

1½ ounces / 15 mL crème de banane
¼ ounce / 7½ mL grenadine
¼ ounce / 7½ mL orgeat syrup
½ ounce / 15 mL heavy cream

Shake and strain into a coupe

– ALLEN R. ROBERTS, USBG COCKTAIL COMPETITION, 1972

Pink Dragon

1 ounce / 30 mL vodka
½ ounce / 15 mL Galliano liqueur
½ ounce / 15 mL crème de noyaux
1 ounce / 30 mL sweet & sour

Shake and strain into a coupe

– LUKE QUAN, USBG COCKTAIL COMPETITION, 1973

Pink Galean

1 ½ ounces / 45 mL light rum
¼ ounce / 7½ mL Galliano liqueur
1 ounce / 30 mL pineapple juice
Dash of grenadine

Shake and strain into a coupe

– RICHARD POUNCE, CBG COCKTAIL COMPETITION, 1968

Pink Haze

1 ounce / 30 mL vodka
½ ounce / 15 mL crème de noyaux
½ ounce / 15 mL Strega liqueur
1 bar spoon of grenadine
1 bar spoon of lemon juice

Stir over ice in a beaker and strain into a coupe

– ANTHONY GIACCO, USBG COCKTAIL COMPETITION, 1974

Pink Mink

1 ounce / 30 mL vodka
¾ ounce / 22½ mL maraschino liqueur
¼ ounce / 7½ mL crème de almond
1 ounce / 30 mL heavy cream

Shake and strain into a coupe

— ALEX SISKO, USBG COCKTAIL COMPETITION, 1973

Pink Princess

1 ounce / 30 mL brandy
¾ ounce / 22½ mL Triple Sec
¼ ounce / 7½ mL crème de almond
½ ounce / 15 mL coconut syrup
¼ ounce / 7½ mL heavy cream

Shake and strain into a coupe

— ALEX SISKO, USBG COCKTAIL COMPETITION, 1974

Pink Velvet

1½ ounces / 45 mL vodka
¾ ounce / 22½ mL Triple Sec
¾ ounce / 22½ mL white crème de cacao
1 ounce / 30 mL coconut juice
1 ounce / 30 mL orange juice
Dash of grenadine

Shake and strain over fresh ice into a tall glass

— ALBERT J. REPETTY, USBG COCKTAIL COMPETITION, 1972

Poco Loco

1½ ounces / 45 mL gold tequila
½ ounce / 15 mL Licor 43
1 ounce / 30 mL orange juice
¼ ounce / 7½ mL prickly pear nectar
Dash of Frothee

Shake and strain into a coupe

— ROBERT "BUDDY" EVATT, USBG COCKTAIL COMPETITION, 1976

Polish Dream

1 ounce / 30 mL vodka
½ ounce / 15 mL dark crème de cacao
½ ounce / 15 mL Triple Sec
1 ounce / 30 mL heavy cream

Shake and strain into a coupe

— CHARLES J. CHOP, USBG COCKTAIL COMPETITION, 1973

Ponce De Leon

1 ounce / 30 mL London dry gin
½ ounce / 15 mL peach liqueur
½ ounce / 15 mL Falernum
½ ounce / 15 mL passion fruit nectar
½ ounce / 15 mL lime juice

Flash blend and pour into a rocks glass half full of crushed ice

— JOE "POPO" GALSINI, CBG COCKTAIL COMPETITION, 1965

Po-Ron Pampero

1 ounce / 30 mL Pampero añejo rum
½ ounce / 15 mL crème de noyaux
¼ ounce / 7½ mL juice 1 lime
Juice of one orange
Splash of carbonated water

Shake the first four ingredients and strain over fresh ice, top with the carbonated water

— JAMIE BAJO, USBG FLORIDA BARTENDERS' GUILD COMPETITION, 1981

Portuguese Peddler

1 ounce / 30 mL blended whiskey
¼ ounce / 7½ mL crème de noyaux
¼ ounce / 7½ mL sweet & sour
2 ounces / 60 mL orange juice
1 barspoon of sugar

Shake and strain over fresh ice into a tall glass

— NICHOLAS KOTSONAS, USBG NATIONAL COCKTAIL COMPETITION, 1974

Princess Lyn

1 ounce / 30 mL Puerto Rican amber rum
½ ounce / 15 mL peach brandy
½ ounce / 15 mL crème de banane
2 ounces / 60 mL orange juice
½ ounce / 15 mL sweet & sour
3 dashes of Frothee

Shake and strain over fresh ice into a tall glass

— AL YCOY, USBG COCKTAIL COMPETITION, 1973

Princess Shel

1 ounce / 30 mL gin
½ ounce / 15 mL Southern Comfort
1 ounce / 30 mL orange juice
2 dashes of maraschino liqueur
2 dashes of orgeat syrup

Shake and strain into a coupe

— RICHARD MASTROSIMONE, CBG COCKTAIL COMPETITION, 1969

Prosita

1 ounce / 30 mL akvavit
1 ounce / 30 mL orange curaçao
1 ounce / 30 mL cranberry juice
1 ounce / 30 mL lemon sour

Shake and strain into a coupe

— EVERETT WILLIAMS, CBG COCKTAIL COMPETITION, 1968

Puamana

¾ ounce / 22½ mL amaretto
¾ ounce / 22½ mL Southern Comfort
1 ounce / 30 mL passion fruit juice
Dash of Mandarine Napoleon
Juice of half a lime

Shake and strain over fresh ice into a tall glass

— EARL TAKASAKI, USBG HAWAII CHAPTER LONG DRINK COCKTAIL COMPETITION, 1983

Pucci's

1 ounce / 30 mL Cognac
½ ounce / 15 mL Triple sec
½ ounce / 15 mL Tuaca Demi-Sec liqueur
½ ounce / 15 mL lemon juice
½ ounce / 15 mL lime juice

Shake and strain into a coupe

— EDWARD GERRARD, CBG COCKTAIL COMPETITION, 1965

Puerto Rico Breeze

1 ounce / 30 mL citrus rum
½ ounce / 15 mL white crème of cacao

Stir over ice in a beaker and strain into a coupe

— ARMANDO RODRIGUEZ, USBG BEFORE DINNER COCKTAIL COMPETITION, 1997

Puma

1 ounce / 30 mL Pampero añejo rum
½ ounce / 15 mL pineapple juice
6 drops grenadine syrup
Top with club soda

Shake and strain over fresh ice into a tall glass

— RAFAEL RODRIGUEZ, USBG FLORIDA BARTENDERS' GUILD COMPETITION, 1981

Red Onion

2 ounces / 60 mL gold tequila
2 dashes of pomegranate syrup
Dash of orgeat syrup
Dash of pepper lime juice*
Dash of limeade

Build over ice in a tall glass
*lime juice with a pinch of coarsely ground black pepper

— JOSE F. ANCONA, CBG COCKTAIL COMPETITION, 1968

Redhead

1¾ ounce / 22½ mL Puerto Rican light rum
¼ ounce / 7½ mL crème de noyaux
1¼ ounce / 40 mL lemon sour
¼ ounce / 7½ mL coconut milk
Dash of Frothee

Shake and strain into a coupe

— IRVIN B. FROST, USBG COCKTAIL COMPETITION, 1972

Rednik

2 ounce / 60 mL Puerto Rican light rum
¼ ounce / 7½ mL crème de noyaux
½ ounce / 15 mL orange curaçao
¼ ounce / 7½ mL pineapple juice
½ ounce / 15 mL lemon sour

Shake and strain over fresh ice into a tall glass

— KENNETH RED HARDY, CBG COCKTAIL COMPETITION, 1969

Renzo's Dream

1 ounce / 30 mL white rum
½ ounce / 15 mL pineapple coconut
2 ounces / pineapple juice
1 ounce / 30 mL piña colada mix
Dash of grenadine

Shake and strain over fresh ice into a tall glass

— CESAR SANDOVAL, USBG COCKTAIL COMPETITION, 1999

Rhonda's Dream

1 ounce / 30 mL vodka
¾ ounce / 22½ mL Midori liqueur
¼ ounce / 7½ mL Mandarine Napoleon
¾ ounce / 22½ mL sweet & sour
¼ ounce / 7½ mL heavy cream

Blend with ice and serve in a tall glass

— CLAYTON TOM, USBG HAWAII CHAPTER LONG DINNER DRINK COCKTAIL COMPETITION, 1983

Road Runner

1½ ounce / 45 mL vodka
½ ounce / 15 mL amaretto
1 ounce / 30 mL coconut juice

Shake and strain into a coupe

— AL ARTEAGA, USBG COCKTAIL COMPETITION, 1976

Roasted Russian

1½ ounces / 45 mL coffee flavored vodka
½ ounce / 15 mL amaretto
½ ounce / 15 mL Irish cream

Shake and strain into a coupe

— VINCE CISNEROS, USBG BEFORE DINNER COCKTAIL COMPETITION, 1997

Roberta

1½ ounces / 15 mL Cognac
½ ounce / 15 mL Mandarine Napoleon
twist lemon peel and discard

Stir over ice in a beaker and strain into a coupe

— ROBERT WEALL, USBG HAWAII CHAPTER BEFORE DINNER DRINK COCKTAIL COMPETITION, 1983

Robin

1 ounce / 30 mL vodka
½ ounce / 15 mL Southern Comfort
¼ ounce / 7½ mL crème de almond
½ ounce / 15 mL lemon juice
¼ ounce / 7½ mL orange juice
Dash of orgeat syrup

Shake and strain into a coupe

— JOHN A. RETTINO, CBG COCKTAIL COMPETITION, 1967

Rose Blossom

1 ounce / 30 mL gin
½ ounce / 15 mL crème de noyaux
¾ ounce / 22 ½ mL pineapple juice
¼ ounce / 7½ mL lemon juice
¼ ounce / 7½ mL rock candy syrup

Shake and strain into a coupe

— GEORGE SPERDAKOS, CBG COCKTAIL COMPETITION, 1970

Rose Royce

1 ounce / 30 mL brandy
½ ounce / 15 mL Tuaca liqueur
½ ounce / 15 mL grenadine
½ ounce / 15 mL heavy cream

Shake and strain into a coupe

— EARL RANGEL, USBG COCKTAIL COMPETITION, 1974

Rum Passion

1 ounce / 30 mL white rum
1 ounce / 30 mL mango passion
½ ounce / 15 mL raspberry liqueur
1 ounce / 30 mL sweet & sour
3 ounces / 90 mL club soda

Build over ice in a tall glass

— ARTURO A. PEINADO, USBG COCKTAIL COMPETITION, 1999

Rum Runner

1 ounce / 30 mL Puerto Rican light rum
½ ounce / 15 mL Southern Comfort
¼ ounce / 7½ mL crème de noyaux
¼ ounce / 7½ mL orgeat syrup
1 ounce / 30 mL orange juice
½ ounce / 15 mL lemon juice

Shake and strain over fresh ice into a tall glass

— JOHN A. RETTINO, CBG COCKTAIL COMPETITION, 1969

Rum-Ba

¾ ounce // 22½ mL dark rum
¼ ounce / 7½ mL banana liqueur
¼ ounce / 7½ mL Triple Sec
1½ ounce / 45 mL sweet & sour

Shake and strain into a coupe

— ANTONIO E. ANCONA, USBG BEFORE DINNER COCKTAIL COMPETITION, 1997

Rusty Dusty

1 ounce / 30 mL apricot brandy
½ ounce / 15 mL Cointreau
1 ounce / 30 mL lemon sour
Dash of Frothee

Shake and strain into a coupe

— JACK T. SHERWOOD, USBG COCKTAIL COMPETITION, 1972

Sam's #1

1 ounce / 30 mL vodka
¾ ounce / 22½ mL crème de banane
¾ ounce / 22½ mL orange juice
1 ounce / 30 mL coconut juice
Dash of grenadine

Shake and strain into a coupe

— ROBERT KOEN, CBG COCKTAIL COMPETITION, 1968

Sam's #2

1 ounce / 30 mL brandy
½ ounce / 15 mL crème de banane
½ ounce / 15 mL orange juice
1 ounce / 30 mL coconut juice
Dash of grenadine

Shake and strain into a coupe

— ROBERT KOEN, CBG COCKTAIL COMPETITION, 1969

Sand Piper

1 ounce / 30 mL tequila
¾ ounce / 22½ mL Tuaca liqueur
¼ ounce / 7½ mL grenadine
1 ounce / 30 mL heavy cream

Shake and strain into a coupe

— EARL RANGEL, USBG COCKTAIL COMPETITION, 1973

Sapphire

1 ounce / 30 mL brandy
¾ ounce / 22½ mL blue curaçao
¾ ounce / 22½ mL lemon sour
1 ounce / 30 mL coconut Milk

Shake and strain into a coupe

— JOSEPH COMELLA, CBG COCKTAIL COMPETITION, 1967

Satin Doll

1 ounce / 30 mL vodka
½ ounce / 15 mL Triple Sec
½ ounce / 15 mL crème de banane
1 ounce / 30 mL lemon juice

Shake and strain into a coupe

— JOHN W. CHOP, CBG COCKTAIL COMPETITION, 1965

Satin Glow

1 ¼ ounce / 40 mL gin
¼ ounce / 7½ mL crème de banane
1 ounce / 30 mL orange juice
½ ounce / 15 mL pineapple juice

Shake and strain into a coupe

— NICHOLAS KOTSONAS, CBG COCKTAIL COMPETITION, 1968

Satin Sheets

1 ounce / 30 mL Puerto Rican silver rum
¾ ounce / 22½ mL Galliano liqueur
¼ ounce / 7½ mL grenadine
1 ounce / 30 mL heavy cream

Shake and strain into a coupe

— **JACK T. SHERWOOD, USBG COCKTAIL COMPETITION, 1973**

Saturn

1 ½ ounce / 45 mL dry gin
½ ounce / 15 mL passion fruit nectar
½ ounce / 15 mL lime juice (also listed with lemon juice)
¼ ounce / 7½ mL simple syrup
¼ ounce / 7½ mL Falernum
¼ ounce / 7½ mL orgeat syrup

Flash blend and pour into a rocks glass half full of crushed ice; Garnish with a cocktail cherry and a lemon wheel on a pick

— **JOE "POPO" GALSINI, CBG COCKTAIL COMPETITION, 1967**

Saturn #2

2 ounces / 60 mL gin
½ ounce / 15 mL orange curaçao
½ ounce / 15 mL sweet vermouth

Stir over ice in a beaker and strain into a coupe
Garnish with a twist of an orange peel

— **JOE "POPO" GALSINI, CBG COCKTAIL COMPETITION, 1968**

Scotch Frog

2 ounce / 60 mL vodka
½ ounce / 15 mL Galliano liqueur
½ ounce / 15 mL Cointreau
Juice of ½ lime
Dash of Angostura bitters

Shake with cracked ice and strain into a coupe

— **ALBIN FARLEY, UKBG–USA WEST COAST COCKTAIL COMPETITION, 1957**

Scotch Kist

1 ounce / 30 mL blended Scotch whisky
½ ounce / 15 mL Grand Tully liqueur
½ ounce / 15 mL Falernum
1 ounce / 30 mL orange juice

Shake and strain into a coupe

— **LOUIS ESCOBEDO, CBG COCKTAIL COMPETITION, 1967**

Secret Harbor

1 ounce / 30 mL Puerto Rican light rum
½ ounce / 15 mL orange curaçao
½ ounce / 15 mL Galliano liqueur
1 barspoon Myers's rum
1 ounce / 30 mL orange juice
½ ounce / 15 mL lime juice

Shake and strain over fresh ice into a tall glass

— **LEONARD "LENNY" CASTEEL, CBG COCKTAIL COMPETITION, 1965**

Sexy Marie

½ ounce / 15 mL 1992 LBV Port
¾ ounce / 22½ mL banana strawberry liqueur
¾ ounce / 22½ mL pineapple coconut liqueur
¼ ounce / 7½ mL melon liqueur
2¼ ounces / 7½ mL pineapple juice

Shake and strain over ice into a tall glass

— **WILLIE LEE, USBG COCKTAIL COMPETITION, 1999**

Silver Nut

1 ounce / 30 mL Hawaiian white rum
¾ ounce / 22½ mL macadamia nut liqueur
½ ounce / 15 mL melon liqueur
¾ ounce / 22 ½ mL sweet & sour
1 ounce / 30 mL orange juice

Shake and strain over fresh ice into a tall glass
Garnish with an orange wheel and a cocktail cherry

— **CLAYTON TOM, HAWAII CHAPTER LONG DRINK COCKTAIL COMPETITION, 1983**

Skipperette

1½ ounces / 45 mL Cognac
½ ounce / 15 mL apricot brandy
½ ounce / 15 mL Southern Comfort
¼ ounce / 7½ mL orgeat syrup
1 ounce / 30 mL pineapple juice

No mixing instructions were listed

— **CARL SWANSON, USBG COCKTAIL COMPETITION, 1965**

Skyliner

1½ ounces / 45 mL American brandy
½ ounce / 15 mL amaretto
3 ounces / 120 mL ginger ale

Build over ice in a tall glass

— **ROBERT G. IVERSON, USBG NATIONAL COCKTAIL COMPETITION**

Slow Maggie

1½ ounces / 45 mL gold tequila
½ ounce / 15 mL Triple Sec
½ ounce / 15 mL sloe gin
1 ounce / 30 mL lemon juice
Dash of Frothee

Shake and strain into a coupe

— **RICHARD SANSONE, USBG COCKTAIL COMPETITION, 1976**

Sonora Cocktail

1 ounce / 30 mL Southern Comfort
½ ounce /15 mL tequila
1 ounce / 30 mL orange juice
3 drops of Frothee

Shake and strain into a coupe

— **JOSE C. RUISECO, USBG COCKTAIL COMPETITION, 1972**

Sonora Sneak

1½ ounces / 45 mL tequila
¼ ounce / 7½ mL Licor 43
2 ounces / 60 mL orange juice
2 ounces / 60 mL sweet & sour
½ ounce / 15 mL prickly pear nectar

Shake and strain over fresh ice into a tall glass

— RICHARD "BUDDY" EVATT, USBG NATIONAL COCKTAIL COMPETITION, 1974

Spanish Gold

1 ounce / 30 mL tequila
½ ounce / 5 mL Licor 43
1½ ounce / 45 mL heavy cream

Shake and strain into a coupe

— EDWARD VANCE, USBG COCKTAIL COMPETITION, 1974

Spanish Kiss

1 ounce / 30 mL brandy
½ ounce / 15 mL Kahlua
½ ounce / 15 mL crème de banane
1 ounce / 30 mL heavy cream

Shake and strain into a coupe

— RICHARD (BUD) EVATT, USBG COCKTAIL COMPETITION 1973

Special 69

1½ ounces / 45 mL Pampero rum
½ ounce / 15 mL Licor 43
1 ounce / 30 mL pineapple juice unsweetened

Shake and strain into a coupe

— ANGEL VILLAR, USBG FLORIDA BARTENDERS' GUILD COMPETITION, 1981

Special Lady

1½ ounces / 45 mL light rum
½ ounce / 15 mL crème de almond
1 ounce / 30 mL pineapple juice

Shake and strain into a coupe

— CAESAR SANDOVAL, USBG COCKTAIL COMPETITION, 1980

Spider's Web

1½ ounces / 45 mL blended Scotch whisky
¾ ounce / 22½ mL apricot brandy
½ ounce / 15 mL lemon juice
½ ounce / 15 mL mL orange juice

Shake and strain into a coupe

— EGIDIO "ANGUS" ANGEROSA — FOUNDER OF THE UKBG–USA CHAPTER, 1930S

Stiletto

1¾ ounces / 22½ mL vodka
¼ ounce / 7½ mL Pernod & Fils liqueur

Stir over ice in a beaker and strain into a coupe
Garnish with a lemon twist

— COLIN L. BULLARD, USBG HAWAII CHAPTER BEFORE DINNER COCKTAIL COMPETITION, 1983

Stink Okole

1½ ounces / 45 mL silver rum
¼ ounce / 7½ mL amaretto
½ ounce / 15 mL crème de banane
1½ ounces / 45 mL sweet & sour
½ ounce / 15 mL orange juice

Shake and strain over fresh ice into a tall glass
Garnish with a slice of pineapple, cherry, and orchid

— ALLAN NAGAMINE, USBG HAWAII CHAPTER LONG DRINK COMPETITION, 1983

Strawberry Blond

¾ ounce / 22½ mL brandy
½ ounce / 15 mL strawberry liqueur
¼ ounce / 7½ mL white crème de cacao
1½ ounces / 45 mL heavy cream

Shake and strain into a coupe

— RAY BARRIENTOS, USBG COCKTAIL COMPETITION, 1973

Sun Kiss

1 ounce / 30 mL brandy
½ ounce / 15 mL Galliano liqueur
½ ounce / 15 mL amaretto

Stir over ice in a beaker and strain into a coupe
Garnish with a cocktail cherry

— TITO LEDDA, USBG HAWAII CHAPTER BEFORE DINNER COCKTAIL COMPETITION, 1983

Sun Life

¾ ounce / 22½ mL brandy
¾ ounce / 22½ mL orange curaçao
¾ ounce / 22½ mL pineapple juice
¾ ounce / 22½ mL heavy cream

Stir a beaker and strain over ice into a rocks glass

— JOHN J. GILBERT, USBG COCKTAIL COMPETITION, 1972

Sundor

1½ ounces / 45 mL Suntory whisky
½ ounce / 15 mL melon liqueur
¼ ounce / 7½ mL dry vermouth

Stir over ice in a beaker and strain into a coupe

— LYLE H. GORDON, USBG BEFORE DINNER COCKTAIL COMPETITION, 1997

Sweet-Peach

1 ounce / 30 mL wilderberry schnapps
1 ounce / 30 mL white chocolate liqueur
½ ounce / 15 mL heavy cream

Blend with ice and pour into a coupe

— PHIL KIRROS, USBG BEFORE DINNER COCKTAIL COMPETITION, 1997

Sylvia's Dream

1 ounce / 30 mL Puerto Rican amber rum
½ ounce / 15 mL crème de banane
½ ounce / 15 mL amaretto
1 ounce / 30 mL heavy cream

Shake and strain into a coupe

— JOHN E. RETTINO, USBG COCKTAIL COMPETITION, 1973

Tea By George

1½ ounce / 45 mL Suntory green tea
¾ ounce / 22½ mL Cointreau
1 ounce / 30 mL heavy cream

Shake and strain into a coupe

— GEORGE C. SPERDAKOS, USBG COCKTAIL COMPETITIONS, 1972

Tempo

1 ounce / 30 mL gin
½ ounce / 15 mL crème de banane
½ ounce / 15 mL Falernum
½ ounce / 15 mL passion fruit nectar
1 ounce / 30 mL orange juice

Flash blend and pour into a rocks glass half full of crushed ice

— JOE "POPO" GALSINI, CBG COCKTAIL COMPETITION, 1970

Tequaize

1 ounce / 30 mL blanco tequila
1 ounce / 30 mL watermelon liqueur
½ ounce / 15 mL mango passion fruit
1 ounce / 30 mL sweet & sour
1 ounce / 30 mL pineapple juice

Build over ice in a tall glass

— JOHN POSELLA, USBG COCKTAIL COMPETITION, 1999

Think Campero

2 ounce / 60 mL añejo rum
1 ounce / 30 mL Licor 43
¼ ounce / 7½ mL sloe gin
2 ounce / 60 mL lemon juice

Shake and strain over fresh ice into a tall glass

— CARLOS BELLO, USBG NATIONAL LONG DRINK COMPETITION, 1983

Tinker Bell

1½ ounce / 45 mL gin
¼ ounce / 7½ mL Grand Marnier
¼ ounce / 7½ mL apricot brandy
½ ounce / 15 mL lemon juice
½ ounce / 15 mL orange juice

Shake and strain into a coupe

— NORMAN TOON, CBG COCKTAIL COMPETITION, 1968

Tio Popo

1 ounce / 30 mL Puerto Rican silver rum
½ ounce / 15 mL apricot brandy
¼ ounce / 7½ mL Falernum
¼ ounce / 7½ mL passion fruit nectar
1 ounce / 30 mL orange juice
Dash of Frothee

Flash blend and pour into a rocks glass half full of crushed ice

— JOE "POPO" GALSINI, USBG COCKTAIL COMPETITION, 1971

Tipsy

1½ ounce / 45 mL Puerto Rican silver rum
½ ounce / 15 mL Suntory Cherry Blossom liqueur
½ ounce / 15 mL Galliano liqueur
1 ounce / 30 mL lemon sour
1 ounce / 30 mL orange juice
¼ ounce / 7½ mL orgeat syrup
3 drops of Angostura creamy head

Blend with ice and serve in a tall glass

— VALERIO "BOBBY" BATUGO, USBG MIXED DRINK COMPETITION, 1971

T.K.O. II

1 ounce / 30 mL vodka
¾ ounce / 22½ mL Mandarine Napoléon
¾ ounce / 22½ mL sweet & sour
Dash of Frothee

Shake and strain into a coupe

— VIRGIL TROPEA, USBG COCKTAIL COMPETITION, 1973

Tommy's Margarita

2 ounces / 60 mL 100% agave tequila
1 ounce / 30 mL lime juice
1 ounce / 30 mL agave syrup (50:50)

Shake and dump directly into a rocks glass

— JULIO BERMEJO, CIRCA 1989

Toot

1 ounce / 30 mL vodka
½ ounce / 15 mL Galliano liqueur
1 ounce / 30 mL heavy cream
½ ounce / 15 mL crème de cassis

Shake and strain into a coupe

— OTTO EIGENMANN, USBG COCKTAIL COMPETITION, 1973

Tootsie

1 ounce / 30 mL gin
½ ounce / 15 mL blue curaçao
½ ounce / 15 mL Puerto Rican amber rum
1½ ounce / 45 mL orange juice
1 egg yolk
splash of ginger ale

Shake and strain over fresh ice into a tall glass
Garnish with a slice of orange and a cocktail cherry

— JOSE MANZANO, USBG HAWAII CHAPTER COCKTAIL LONG DRINK COMPETITION, 1983

Top Banana

1½ ounce / 45 mL gin
½ ounce / 15 mL crème de banane
½ ounce / 15 mL cherry brandy
½ ounce / 15 mL orange juice
Dash of lemon juice

Blend with ice and serve in a rocks glass

— JAMES "JIMMY" P. CAMPBELL, CBG COCKTAIL COMPETITION, 1968

Topaze

1 ounce / 30 mL vodka
½ ounce / 15 mL Galliano liqueur
½ ounce / 15 mL Grand Marnier
1 ounce / 30 mL orange juice

Shake and strain into a coupe

— KURT BEHRINGER, CBG COCKTAIL COMPETITION, 1968

Trinidad

1¼ ounces / 45 mL light rum
½ ounce / 15 mL Chococo liqueur
¼ ounce / 7½ mL white crème de menthe
¼ ounce / 7½ mL prickly pear syrup
2 ounces / 60 mL orange juice

Shake and strain over fresh ice into a tall glass

— HAROLD E. ROBINSON, USBG NATIONAL COCKTAIL COMPETITION, 1974

Tuacian

2 ounces / 60 mL Tuaca liqueur
½ ounce / 15 mL Galliano liqueur
¼ ounce / 7½ mL orange curaçao
Juice of ½ lime - drop hull

Shake and strain into a coupe

— PETER ZAMUTO, CBG COCKTAIL COMPETITION, 1974

Universal

2 ounce / 60 mL añejo rum
½ ounce / 15 mL Galliano liqueur
½ ounce / 15 mL crème de banane
1 ounce / 30 mL orange juice
1 ounce / 30 mL pineapple juice

Blend with ice and serve in a tall glass

— NICK KICHUPOLOS, CBG COCKTAIL COMPETITION, 1969

Universe

1 ounce / 30 mL vodka
½ ounce / 15 mL melon Liqueur
½ ounce / 15 mL pistachio liqueur
1½ ounces / 45 mL pineapple juice
½ ounce / 15 mL sweetened lime juice

Shake and pour contents into special tall glass filled with cracked ice
Garnish with a flag or an umbrella, pineapple stick, orange, cocktail cherry, and sprig of fresh mint

— VALERIO "BOBBY" BATUGO, USBG LONG DRINK COMPETITION, 1978

USBG Cocktail

1½ ounces / 45 mL gold tequila
1 ounce / 30 mL Dom Benedictine
1½ ounces / 45 mL sweet & sour
Dash of grenadine

Shake and strain into a coupe

— JOSE F. ANCONA, USBG COCKTAIL COMPETITION, 1971

Valley Orchard

1½ ounces / 45 mL brandy
1 ounce / 30 mL apricot brandy
½ ounce / 15 mL sweet & sour

Shake and strain into a coupe

— ANDREW PAWLAK, CBG COCKTAIL COMPETITION, 1970

Velvet Kiss

1 ounce / 30 mL London dry gin
½ ounce / 15 mL crème de banane
½ ounce / 15 mL pineapple juice
1 ounce / 30 mL heavy cream
Dash of grenadine

Shake and strain into a chilled champagne glass

— ALBERT J. REPETTY, USBG COCKTAIL COMPETITION, 1974

Voderic

1½ ounces / 45 mL vodka
¼ ounce / 7½ mL crème de banane
½ ounce / 15 mL Burgundy
¼ ounce / 7½ mL lime juice

Shake and strain into a coupe

— W. JAKE OHLSEN, USBG COCKTAIL COMPETITION, 1976

Vodka Gimlet Supreme

1 ounce / 30 mL vodka
¾ ounce / 22½ mL peach brandy
¼ ounce / 7½ mL lime juice

Build over ice in a tall glass

— WILLIAM KUHHORN, CBG COCKTAIL COMPETITION, 1968

Volcanic Rumble

1 ounce / 30 mL spiced rum
½ ounce / 15 mL apricot liqueur
½ ounce / 15 mL Galliano liqueur
1 ounce / 30 mL orange juice
cranberry juice to fill

Build over ice in a tall glass

– JACK WILLARD, USBG COCKTAIL COMPETITION, 1999

Warlina

1 ounce / 30 mL light rum
½ ounce / 15 mL Galliano liqueur
½ ounce / 15 mL crème de noyaux
1 ounce / 30 mL sweet & sour
Dash of orgeat syrup
Dash of Frothee

Blend with ice and serve in a tall glass

– VALERIO "BOBBY" BATUGO, USBG MIXED DRINK COMPETITION, 1974

Waterproof

1 ounce / 30 mL Soranzo lemon liqueur
½ ounce / 15 mL Midori
½ ounce / 15 mL crème de banane
½ ounce / 15 mL sweet vermouth
3 drops of grenadine

Shake and strain into a coupe

– JOSE RUISECO, USBG BEFORE DINNER COCKTAIL COMPETITION, 1997

Whiskey Smash

6–8 fresh mint leaves
½ small lemon - quartered and seeded
¾ ounce / 22½ mL simple syrup
2 ounces / 60 mL rye whiskey

Muddle the mint leaves, lemon, and syrup in a chilled cocktail shaker
Add the whiskey and fill the shaker with ice
Shake hard and strain into a small, chilled rocks glass filled with fresh ice
Garnish with a mint sprig

– DALE DEGROFF. POPULARIZED AT EASTERN STANDARD RESTAURANT IN BOSTON (MA), 1998

Winner's Cup

1 ounce / 30 mL vodka
½ ounce / 15 mL crème de banane
½ ounce / 15 mL dark crème de cacao
1 ounce / 30 mL heavy cream

Shake and strain into a coupe

– JOSEPH MINILLO, USBG COCKTAIL COMPETITION, 1974

Zinger

1½ ounce / 45 mL Suntory whisky
½ ounce / 15 mL lime juice
¾ ounce / 22½ Galliano liqueur

Shake and strain into a coupe

– NAOMI FILBURN, USBG BEFORE DINNER COCKTAIL COMPETITION, 1997

BIBLIOGRAPHY

Berry, Jeff, Beachbum Berry Remixed: A Gallery of Tiki Drinks, Slave Labor Books, 2010

Brown Jared & Miller Anistatia, The Deans of Drink, Mixellany Limited, 2013

CBG Cocktail Competition Souvenir Program Book, CBG 1962

CBG Cocktail Competition Souvenir Program Book, CBG 1963

CBG Cocktail Competition Souvenir Program Book, CBG 1964

CBG Cocktail Competition Souvenir Program Book, CBG 1965

CBG Cocktail Competition Souvenir Program Book, CBG 1966

CBG Cocktail Competition Souvenir Program Book, CBG 1968

CBG Cocktail Competition Souvenir Program Book, CBG 1969

CBG Cocktail Competition Souvenir Program Book, CBG 1970

Craddock, Harry. The Savoy Cocktail Book, Constable & Company Ltd., 1930

Grimes William, Straight Up or On the Rocks, North Point Press, 2001

I.B.A., 60 Years On, International Bartenders' Assoc., 2011

Lakeland Ledger, 1959

Press Herald, May 24, 1967

Stenger, Thomas E., Cocktail Bar Reference Manual, USBG, 1971

Tarling, W.J., Café Royale Cocktail Book, Publications from Pall Mall Ltd., 1937

UKBG International Guide to Drinks, UKBG 1971

UKBG International Guide to Drinks, Ebury Press, 2006

UKBG The Bartender, Publications from Pall Mall Ltd., 1953

UKBG-USA West Coast Chapter Competition Results Book, 1951

UKBG-USA West Coast Chapter Competition Results Book, 1952

UKBG-USA West Coast Chapter Competition Results Book, 1953

UKBG-USA West Coast Chapter Competition Souvenir Program Book, 1954

UKBG-USA West Coast Chapter Competition Souvenir Program Book, 1955

UKBG-USA West Coast Chapter Competition Souvenir Program Book, 1956

USBA, Cocktail Competition Program Book, USBA, 1987

USBA, Cocktail Competition Program Book, USBA, 1988

USBA, Cocktail Competition Program Book, USBA, 1989

USBG, Beverage & Bartending Compendium, USBG, 2013

USBG, Cocktail Competition Program Book, USBG, 1971

USBG, Cocktail Competition Program Book, USBG, 1972

USBG, Cocktail Competition Program Book, USBG, 1973

USBG, Cocktail Competition Program Book, USBG, 1974

USBG, Cocktail Competition Program Book, USBG, 1975

USBG, Cocktail Competition Program Book, USBG, 1976

USBG, Cocktail Competition Program Book, USBG, 1977

USBG, Cocktail Competition Program Book, USBG, 1978

USBG, Cocktail Competition Program Book, USBG, 1979

USBG, Cocktail Competition Program Book, USBG, 1980

USBG, Cocktail Competition Program Book, USBG, 1981

USBG, Cocktail Competition Program Book, USBG, 1982

USBG, Cocktail Competition Program Book, USBG, 1984

USBG, Cocktail Competition Program Book, USBG, 1985

Wondrich David, Imbibe!, Penguin Books, 2007

ACKNOWLEDGEMENTS

To my fiancée Amy and my daughter Gabriella: Thank you for your patience and your support as I was losing my mind trying to write this book. I am happy you were by my side while this was going on.

My sincere appreciation goes to Bridget Albert, Charles Joly, Jen Ackrill, Julio Cabrera, Tiffanie Barriere, and Martin Cate for their contributions to this book in creating the six riffed cocktails inspired by past members of the Guild. It was a pleasure to work with you.

A huge thank you to Jose Ancona and Fred Ireton. For the past six years, you have been feeding my need to understand things as they pertain to the history of the Guild: my brain needed answers, and you were extremely helpful in providing them to me. May you rest in cocktails Jose, you are terribly missed.

Thank you to Aaron Gregory Smith, and the entire board of the United States Bartenders' Guild, for believing in me as a writer and in the value of the story of this book. I can come up with hundreds of cocktail writers that are more experienced than me at doing this; the fact that I got to do it is amazing.

To David Nepove for reading my words and fact-checking the stories. Your positive and genuine comments made the workflow so much better. To Tiffany Soles for being a sounding board, to Liz Edwards and Alex Premo, for helping with the collage pages before every chapter; I consider those pages the most telling parts of this book.

Shout out to Caitlin Terry, who made several trips for me to the USBG storage unit in Sacramento to open old program books and provide me with important recipes and pictures to put in the book.

My gratitude to Francine Cohen for your editorial expertise and common-sense suggestions.

Much appreciation goes out to Eric Weiss and Chloe Uglow for laying out such a beautiful book and still being my friends after all the changes. Another thanks to Chloe Uglow for the beautiful book cover.

To Natalie Tremayne, who patiently sketched all the important characters in this book. To Kyle and Rachel Ford from Ford Media Lab for the 6 pictures of the riffed cocktails. You rock! Last, but definitely not least, a huge thank you to Bob Barnes and Kathleen Bodnar for translating this book from "Livio" to English; I am sure there are other people thanking you for this as well.

INDEX

A

A Blizzard Cocktail, 078
A Lulu Cocktail, 078
A Nightcap at Kaimana Beach Cocktail, 050
A Touch of Glass Cocktail, 078
A Touch of Coral Cocktail, 078
A Touch of Jade Cocktail, 078
Abou-Ganim, Tony, VI, 052, 058-059, 066, 067, 085
Acevedo, Pablo L., 102
Acoba, Robert, 082
Ackrill, Jen, VIII, 050
Adam's Mistake Cocktail, 078
Albert, Bridget, VIII, 066, 067
Aldrich, Donald W., 082, 090
Allen, Roberts R., 114
Aloha Cocktail, 079
Ambassador 76 Cocktail, 079
Ambrosia Restaurant 034-035
Anaheim Convention Center, 071
Ancona, Antonio E., 088, 119
Ancona Special Cocktail, 040
Ancona, Jose F., V, VI, 028, 032, 038, 040, 042, 052, 076, 092, 097, 100, 110, 111, 117, 128
Angerosa, Egidio "Angus", 007, 014, 017, 019, 064, 072, 081, 082, 103, 113, 123
Angie's Cocktail Cocktail, 079
Anna's Delight Cocktail, 079
Apollo Cocktail, 079
Apollo #2 Cocktail, 079
Apple Annie Cocktail, 080
A-Ri-Rang Cocktail, 080
Archer, Ferrol, 104
Ariana's Dream Cocktail, 080
Arrowhead Cocktail, 080
Arrowhead Country Club, 068

Arteaga, Al, 064, 076, 118
Astor Place Cocktail, 080
Auburn Cocktail, 080

B

Babylon Red Cocktail, 081
Bacardi-Martini Grand Prix, 038
Bajo, Jaime, 104, 116
Balkan Beauty Cocktail, 081
Balog, William, 096
Baltazar, John R., 064, 078
Bambino Cocktail, 081
Banana Bliss Cocktail, 014-015, 081
Banana Breeze Cocktail, 081
Banana Daiquiri, 050
Bandido Cocktail, 081
Barandrestaurant.com, 023
Barkeeper Union of Austria (ÖBU), 002
Barrientos, Ray, 124
Barriere, Tiffanie, VIII, 024, 131
Bartender Hall of Fame, 068
Bartenders Club of the Republic of Cuba, 002
Batugo, Mario, 061-063, 076
Batugo, Valerio Gamet "Bobby" 013, 044, 047, 060-063, 076, 082, 097, 099, 107, 126, 128, 129
Bavarian Mint Cocktail, 082
Beach, Donn, 013
Beach Music Cocktail, 082
Beechler, John E., 105
Beehler, Nick 064, 076, 088, 092, 098
Behringer, Kurt 047, 065, 076, 080, 127
Belinda Cocktail, 082
Bello, Carlos, 125
Bendinelli, George, 085
Bermejo, Julio, 023, 126
Berner, Charles 023, 076, 082
Bernice Cocktail, 082
Berry, Jeff "Beachbum" 013, 035, 061

Best Year Cocktail, 061, 095
Betty Dighton's Mint Cocktail, 014-015, 082
Beverage Bulletin, 032
Beverage Industry News, 032
Big Daddy Cocktail, 083
Big Mammo Cocktail, 083
Binnacle Cocktail, 083
Bisbois, Ralph, 064
Blue Bird Cocktail, 083
Bluebird Cocktail #2, 083
Blue Cobra Cocktail, 084
Blue Finn Cocktail, 084
Blue Gardenia Cocktail, 084
Blue Heaven Cocktail, 084
Blue Hawaii, 050
Blue Horizon Cocktail, 084
Blue Lagoon Cocktail, 084
Blue Max Cocktail, 085
Bodene, Carole, 064, 070
Bodnar, Kathleen, 065, 131
Bogdan, Dadynski, 107
Bols Royal Distilleries, 001-002
Boob Ala Cocktail, 085
Boom Boom Cocktail, 085
Boomerang Cocktail, 085
Borella, George, 064, 091
Boyd, Fredrick A., 064, 111
Bowman, Frank J., 113
Bradford, William, 065, 102
Breakfast at Sardi's, 061
Britannica.com, 005
Brown, William "Bill", 065, 076, 105, 113
Brown, Fred, 064
Brown, Jared, 007, 010
Brown, William, 078
Bullard, Collin L., 064, 088, 124
Bumble Bee Cocktail, 085
Burton, John C, 064, 072-073

C

C'est Si Bon Cocktail, 086
Cabalar, Ike, 060
Caberto, Rudy, 065
Cable Car Cocktail, 066, 067, 085
Cabrera, Julio, VII, 040
Cabo Azul Cocktail, 086
Café La Maze, 061
Café Royale Cocktail Book, 004-005, 014-015
California Bartenders' Guild (CBG), 031-032, 038, 040, 047-048
Calo, Robert, 084
Campbell, James P., 047, 064, 108, 109, 127
Campos, Normando, 112
Canyon Cocktail, 086
Captain's Inn (tavern), 034
Carmenita Cocktail, 086
Carrillo, Al, 076, 087, 093, 098, 099
Casteel, Leonard "Lenny", 032, 048-049, 065, 072, 109, 121
Cate, Martin, VIII, 036
Cecil's Dream Cocktail, 086
Ceiling Zero Cocktail, 086
Challenge Cup–Team Award, 032
Champ, Clark, 064, 101
Chaplin, Charlie, 060
Chard, Samuel J., 078
Charon, Leroy, 047, 076, 094, 095, 107
China Trader Restaurant, 047
Chococo Joe Cocktail, 087
Chocolate Egg Crème Cocktail, 087
Chocolate Island Cocktail, 087
Chop, Charles J. "Charlie", 028, 044, 047, 052, 070, 076, 078, 081, 083, 115
Chop, John W., 028, 032, 065, 076, 087, 107, 108, 110, 120
Chop Nut Cocktail, 087
Cisneros, Cathy, 064

Cisneros, Vince, 065, 076, 104, 118
Clayton, Tom, 064, 118, 122
Club de Cantineros de Cuba, 002
Chanticleersociety.org, 055
Cleveland Clinic, 003
Coca-Cooler Cocktail, 087
Cocaretto Cocktail, 088
Coco Cocktail, 088
Cocktail (Film), 054
Cocktail Dark ages, 031
Cocktail Rediscovery era, 074
Cocktail Restoration era, 074
Coconut Breeze Cocktail, 088
Cognac Matinee Cocktail, 088
Cognac Perino Cocktail, 088
Coleman, Ada, 008
Coleman, Walter, 065
Colonial Restaurant, 017
Colona, William J., 113
Colored Citizen, The, Newspaper, 024
Comella, Joseph, 120
Cormier, Phillip, 046, 065, 080, 088
Conklin, Al, 064, 112
Cool-One Cocktail, 089
Cool Lagoon Cocktail, 089
Coolik, Eugene, 092
Cordero, Anthony V., 088, 095, 106, 114
Cormier, Philip A., 080, 098
Cornuke, Paul Jr., 083, 084, 096
Corpse Reviver #2 Cocktail, 009, 089
Cracklin' Rose Cocktail, 089
Craddock, Harry, 004, 006-008

D

Daily.jstor.org, 071
Danish Fruit Cocktail, 089
De La Fuente, Max, 065, 103
Dean, James, 062
Decker, Kenneth, 065, 089, 097

DeGroff, Dale VI, 057-058, 129
De La Liata, Oscar, 106, 113
DeLong, J. Bradford, 001
Derby Winner Cocktail, 090
Desert Breeze Cocktail, 090
Difford's Guide, 008
Dimy's Baby Cocktail, 090
Disneyland Hotel, 034
Dodd, Wes, 065
Dolce Vita Cocktail, 090
Don Calypso Cocktail, 090
Dorland Hall, 007
Downtown Cocktail, 090
Drinkboy.com, 058
Duff, John Jr., 101
Dukerich, Sean, 065, 110
Durlesser, John "Johnny", 019, 021-023, 064, 073, 076, 102, 106
Dust Bowl, 001-003
Dutch Kist Cocktail, 091

E

Ed's Baby Cocktail, 091
Edwards, F., 006-007
Eigenmann, Otto, 108, 126
El Boss Cocktail, 091
El Dante Cocktail, 091
El Diablo Cocktail, 019
El Picador Cocktail, 023
Ellis, Tobin, 056
Entrepid Cocktail, 091
Escobedo, Louis, 091, 121
Evatt, Richard "Buddy", 115, 123
Evening's Delight Cocktail, 092

F

Fantastic Cocktail, 092
Farley, Al, 076, 121
Ferguson, Cody, 042

Ferrer, Carmen, 083
Filburn, Naomi, 052, 065, 070-071, 087, 129
Filipino Bartenders, 032, 034
Finn And Fran Cocktail, 092
Finney, Jack P., 017, 019
First Blush Cocktail, 092
Flair Bartending, 056
Flamingo Cocktail, 092
Flores, Melissa, 032
Foat, Raymond, 065
Fontana, Alfredo, 069, 100, 112
FoodandWine.com, 002
Ford, Henry, 001
Fran-Daddy Cocktail, 092
French Kiss Cocktail, 093
Frost, Irvin B., 064, 117
Frosty Dawn Cocktail, 093
Frosty Emerald Cocktail, 093
Fructuoso, Prado, 080
Funky Monkey Cocktail, 093

G

Galsini, José Valencia, Joe "Popo", 019-020, 033-034, 064, 076, 084, 114, 115, 121, 125, 126
Geine Cocktail, 093
Gemini 13 Cocktail, 093
Gentry, Ted, 084
Gerrard, Edward, 117
Giacco, Anthony "Buddy", 064, 070, 114
Gigi Cocktail, 094
Glibert, John J., 104, 124
Gindori Cocktail, 094
Giuliani, Vincent, 065, 106
Glide'er Cocktail, 094
Gold Swan Cocktail, 094
Gold Snake Cocktail, 094
Golden Aggie Cocktail, 094
Golden Amber Cocktail, 095
Golden Comet Cocktail, 095

Golden Dream Cocktail, 095
Golden Perino Cocktail, 095
Golden Perino #2 Cocktail, 095
Golden Princess Cocktail, 095
Golden Star Cocktail, 095
Golden Tail Cocktail, 096
Golden Touch Cocktail, 096
Golden Trader Cocktail, 096
Golden Turtle Cocktail, 096
Golden Wave Cocktail, 096
Golden Wench, 097
Gonzalez, Felipe, 091, 105
Gordon, Lyle H., 064, 078, 097, 124
Gordon, Robert, 101, 106
Granada Cocktail, 097
Green Eyes Cocktail, 097
Green Wave Cocktail, 097
Great Depression, The, 001-002
Gypsy Cocktail, 097

H

H.D. Davies & Co, 019
Hanson, Web, 017, 019
Hanky Panky, 008
Hardy, Kenneth Red, 117
Harris, Homer, 023
Harroll, Horrace, 024
Hartung, Ervin Sr., 090
Heaven Cocktail, 097
Henry's Restaurant, 068
Hess, Robert, 058
Hey Panco Cocktail, 098
Hi-Fi Cocktail, 098
High Tide Cocktail, 098
Ho, Don, 050
Ho, K.Y. Sam, 065, 099
Hody's Restaurant, 014
Hody's Misty Cocktail, 098
Hoffman House, 008

Holland House, 008
Honey Bear Cocktail, 098
Honey Berry Cocktail, 098
Honeymoon Cocktail, 099
Hooker of 76 Cocktail, 077, 099
Hornet Cocktail, 099
Hukilau Polynesian Lounge, 034
Hulbert, Jason, 112
Hutchison, Edward, 064

I

Icy Sea Cocktail, 099
Inc.com, 070
Industrial Revolution, 001
Innocent Eyes Cocktail, 099
International Barkeepers Union (IBU), 001
International Bartenders' Association (IBA), 007, 031, 056
International Cocktail Competition (ICC), 048, 068
International Spice Cocktail, 099
Ireton, Fred, 016, 019, 053, 058, 064, 068, 070, 072, 073, 076, 082, 092, 109
Irish Affair Cocktail, 100
Irish Greek Cocktail, 100
Irish Rover Cocktail, 100
Irish Smash Cocktail, 100
Island Sunset Cocktail, 100
issuu.com, 007
Iverson, Robert, 065, 076, 078, 084, 122

J

Jealousy Cocktail, 100
Jewel's Delight Cocktail, 101
Johnson, Harry, 073
Johnson, Judy, 065
Jojo Lou Cocktail, 101
Jojo Lou The II Cocktail, 101
Joly, Charles, VIII, 026

Jones, Danny, 093
Jones, Jimmy, 064
Jones, Virgel H., 047, 052, 065, 076, 085, 089, 100, 112
Jose Cuervo Tequila, 021-022
Jose's Siesta Cocktail, 101

K

Ka Va Cocktail, 101
Kanelos, Nick, 100
Kay's Kooler Cocktail, 101
Keale, Moe, 050
Kehl, Jerry, 103
Kelbo's, 034
Kentucky Sunset Cocktail, 102
Kesha Cocktail, 102
Key Club (lounge), 061
Kichupolos, Nick, 127
Kim Cocktail, 102
Kim, George, 076
King Edward Cocktail, 102
Kirros, Phil, 065, 093, 125
Kitchupolos, Nick, 065, 098
Knickerbocker Hotel, 008
Koen, Robert, 094, 096, 120
Kona Kai Restaurant, 034
Kool Banana Cocktail, 102
Kotsonas, Nicholas, 065, 076, 116, 120
Kuhhorn, William, 128

L

Ladies Pampero Cocktail, 103
Lafranconi, Francesco, 052-053, 059
Lancer Cocktail, 104
Latimes.com, 068
Latin Lace Cocktail, 104
La Vita Doucke Cocktail, 102
Ledda, Rositito "Tito", 050, 065, 076, 111, 124
Lee, Willie, 081, 122

Leg Before Wicket Cocktail, 014-015, 103
Leung, Howard, 079
Levy, Gil, 103
Lifetime Member Award, 071
Lightner, Kelly, 048, 065, 076, 106
Lily Cocktail, 103
Linda Lou Cocktail, 103
Little Cooler Cocktail, 104
Loftin, Bronson, 042
Long Beach Shake Cocktail, 104
Long Beach Yacht Club, 068
Long, Garnet H., 081
Lost Streaker Cocktail, 104
Louise Cocktail, 104
Lovefood.com, 002
Lovely Lady Cocktail, 104
Lovers' Kiss Cocktail, 104
Lowther, Smith, 065, 083
Lu Cocktail, 105
Lu II Cocktail, 105
Lucky Concoction Cocktail, 105
Luxury Cocktail, 026, 105
Luxury Cocktail #2, 026
Lynch, Max, 065, 085

M

Macarena Cocktail, 105
Magic Castle Cocktail, 105
Magro, Jess, 093, 104
Mai Tai 019,
Malibu Orchid Cocktail, 106
Malla Cocktail, 106
Malta, Thomas, 047, 065, 086, 099
Manzanita Cocktail, 106
Manzano, Jose, 065, 109, 127
Maple Leaf Cocktail, 106
Marbach, Phil, 079
Margarita cocktail, 021, 023, 106
Martinee Cocktail Cocktail, 106

Martinez, Raymundo B., 100
Mary Rose Cocktail, 107
Mastrosimone, Richard, 095, 116
McCann, James P., 111
McGuinness, Althea, 062
McHenry's Tail O' the Cock, 022
McKeon, William, 093
McLaughlin, Jack, 080
McNeely, C, 044
Meaney, Joseph C., 087
Mellow Yellow Cocktail, 107
Melonaire Cocktail, 107
Melotini Cocktail, 107
Memmories Cocktail, 061, 107
Merry Jo Cocktail, 107
Merry K Cocktail, 108
Messmer, William, 065, 079
Mexitalian Cocktail, 108
Midnight Express Cocktail, 108
Midnight Sun Cocktail, 108
Miller, Anistatia, 007, 010
Miller, Philo, 065
Minillo, Joseph, 129
Miss Marnie Cocktail, 108
Miss Marnie #2 Cocktail, 108
Miss Marnie #3 Cocktail, 109
Misty Cocktail, 109
Misty Breeze Cocktail, 109
Misty Miss Cocktail, 109
Molly Brown Cocktail, 109
Moonglow Cocktail, 110
Morton, Shirley, 110
Morton's Delight Cocktail, 110
Moscow Mule, 019
Mouvet, Patrick, 111
MS Cocktail, 110
Muddy Mango Cocktail, 110
Muncy, Russell, 065, 076
My Diane Cocktail, 110

My Dream Cocktail, 111
My Julie Cocktail, 111

N

Nagamine, Allan, 124
Nancy's Fancy Cocktail, 111
Natasha Princess Cocktail, 111
National Archives, 002
Negroni Cocktail, VIII, 047
Neil's Pasta & Seafood Grill, 038
Nepove, David, 071
Ngamine, Allan, 081
Nielsen, Ayoe, 111
Night Cap Cocktail, 050, 111
Nordsiek, Edward F., 019, 064, 076-077, 086, 091, 102

O

O'Brien, Edward D., 064, 092, 101
Ohlsen, Jake W., 100, 128
On The Green Cocktail, 111
Orange Coast Cocktail, 112
Orange Glo Cocktail, 112
O'Shea, Dan, 064, 086
O'Suzanna Cocktail, 112
Outrigger Tiki Bar, 034

P

Pagans Explosion Cocktail, 112
Pampero Dream Cocktail, 112
Pandora Cocktail, 112
Parker, Theodore G., 090
Passion Ora Cocktail, 113
Patrician Cocktail Cocktail, 113
Patrick, Bryan, William, 103, 110
Patti-Lu Cocktail, 113
Paul, Bernard, 007
Pawlak, Andrew, 064, 128
Pazazz Cocktail, 113

Peach Blossom Cocktail, 113
Peach Fuzz Cocktail, 113
Peinado, Arturo, A, 064, 094, 119
Perino Cup Cocktail, 114
Petake (aka Pikake) cocktail, 034, 114
Pelican Club, 017
Perpetual trophy, 033
Person of the Year Award, 070
Picchi, Luca, VIII
Pimm's Restaurant, 017, 019
Pimms No 1, 019, 020
Pink Banana Cocktail, 114
Pink Dragon Cocktail, 114
Pink Galean Cocktail, 114
Pink Haze Cocktail, 114
Pink Mink Cocktail, 115
Pink Princess Cocktail, 115
Pink Velvet Cocktail, 115
Pisano, Shirlee, 052, 065
Poco Loco Cocktail, 115
Policastro, Santiago "Pichin", 049
Polish Dream Cocktail, 115
Ponce De Leon Cocktail, 115
Pounce, Richard, 079, 103
Po-Ron Pampero Cocktail, 116
Portuguese Peddler Cocktail, 116
Posella, John, 125
Pozo, Richie, 048
Prado, Fructuoso, 076
Presley, Elvis, 050
Princess Shel Cocktail, 116
Processed Foods, 002, 012
Pounce, Richard, 114
Prohibition and Repeal, 002, 004, 008, 012, 061-062
Princess Lyn Cocktail, 116
Prosita Cocktail, 116
Puamana Cocktail, 116
Pucci's Cocktail, 117

138

Puerto Rico Breeze Cocktail, 117
Puma Cocktail, 117

Q
Quan, Luke, 084, 114

R
Rangel, Earl, 119, 120
Rapetti, Luca, 019
Raymond, William "Bill", 073
Rea, Brian F., 064, 072-073, 104
Red Onion Cocktail, 117
Redhead Cocktail, 117
Rednik Cocktail, 117
Reed, Claire L., 064, 099
Regan, Gary "Gaz", 008
Renzo's Dream Cocktail, 118
Rhonda's Dream Cocktail, 118
Repetty, Albert J., 064, 076, 093, 097, 098, 099, 102, 115, 128
Rettino, John A., 044, 064, 087, 090, 091, 118, 119, 125
Revere House Restaurant, 070
Road Runner Cocktail, 118
Roasted Russian Cocktail, 118
Roberta Cocktail, 118
Roberts, Marsha, 070
Robin Cocktail, 118
Robinson, Harold E., 127
Rodriquez, Armando, 095, 117
Rodriguez, Emilio, 064
Rodriguez, Rafael, 117
Rose Blossom Cocktail, 119
Rose Royce Cocktail, 119
Rovner, Sam, 065
Ruiseco, Jose, 028, 065, 076, 081, 105, 122, 129
Rum Passion Cocktail, 119
Rum Runner Cocktail, 076, 119
Rum-Ba Cocktail, 119

Rusty Dusty Cocktail, 119
Rychly, James, 079

S
Sam's #1 Cocktail, 120
Sam's #2 Cocktail, 120
Sand Piper Cocktail, 120
Sandoval, Caesar, 071, 076, 086, 118, 123
Sansone, Richard, 065, 122
Santa Ana Elks Lodge, 068
Sapphire Cocktail, 120
Sardi's Restaurant, 061
Satin Doll Cocktail, 120
Satin Glow Cocktail, 120
Satin Sheets Cocktail, 121
Saturn Cocktail, 034-036, 77, 121
Saturn #2 Cocktail, 002, 077, 121
Save the Saturn Society, 036
Savoy Cocktail Book, 004
Savoy Hotel, 008
Scandia Restaurant, 019-020
Schmidt, John, 064
Scotch Frog Cocktail, 121
Scotch Kist Cocktail, 121
Scvhistory.com, 070
Secret Harbor Cocktail, 121
Seeber, Kevin, 008, 013
Sexy Marie Cocktail, 122
Sherwood, Jack T., 076, 119, 121
Silverman, Milt, 065
Silver Nut Cocktail, 122
Simpson, Walter, 026, 076, 105
Sisko, Alex, 115
Skipperette Cocktail, 122
Sky Ranch Foundation, 032
Skyliner Cocktail, 122
Slow Maggie Cocktail, 122
Smith, Carmen, 070
Smuggler's Cove, 036

Sonora Cocktail Cocktail, 122
Sonora Sneak Cocktail, 123
Spanish Flu, IX
Spanish Gold Cocktail, 123
Spanish Kiss Cocktail, 123
Speakeasy, 002
Spear, Alan D., 109
Special 69 Cocktail, 123
Special Lady Cocktail, 123
Sperdakos, George, 064, 085, 119, 125
Spider's Web Cocktail, 014-015, 123
Stambaugh, Patrick J., 078
Star of Earth Cocktail, 036
Steller, M, 044
Stenger, Tom, 065, 072, 076, 108
Stern's Famous BBQ, 014, 019
Stiletto Cocktail, 124
Stink Okole Cocktail, 124
Stocker, David, 094, 097
Stokes, David, 024
Strawberry Blond Cocktail, 124
Sullivan, Robert, 107
Sun-kissed Margarita, 024
Sun Kiss Cocktail, 124
Sun Life Cocktail, 124
Sundor Cocktail, 124
Supnet, Benny, 064
Supnet, Rick, 065, 090
Surf & Sand Hotel, 034
Swanson, Carl, 086, 094, 122
Swanson, Ray, 044, 101
Sweet-Peach Cocktail, 125
Swinney, Al, 064
Swiss Barkeeper Union, 002
Sword, David L., 089
Sylvia's Dream Cocktail, 125

T

Takahashi, Ricky, 065

Takasaki, Earl, 065, 086, 116
Tam O'Shanter (tavern), 017
Tamashiro, Brian, 064
Tarling, William "Bill", 004, 006, 083
Tea By George Cocktail, 125
Tempo Cocktail, 125
Tequaize Cocktail, 125
The Deans of Drinks, 007
The Islands Bar, 034
Think Campero Cocktail, 125
Thomas, Jerry, 007
Tiki, 013, 034
Tinker Bell Cocktail, 126
Tio Popo Cocktail, 126
Tip's Jardine, 061 – 062
Tipsy Cocktail, 126
T'K.O. II Cocktail, 126
Tommy's Margarita, 023, 126
Toon, Norman, 065, 126
Toot Cocktail, 126
Tootsie Cocktail, 127
Top Banana Cocktail, 127
Top of Waikiki Restaurant, 050
Topaze Cocktail, 127
Trinidad Cocktail, 127
Tropea, Virgil, 089, 102, 109
Tuacian Cocktail, 127
Tulsaworld.com, 031
Tropical Itch Cocktail, 050

U

UKBG-USA East Coast Bartenders' Guild, 019, 073
UKBG-USA West Coast Bartenders' Guild, 018-020, 031, 034
Underwood, Vern, 022
United Kingdom Bartenders' Guild (UKBG), 02, 04, 07, 014, 017, 031
Universal Cocktail, 127

Puerto Rico Breeze Cocktail, 117
Puma Cocktail, 117

Q

Quan, Luke, 084, 114

R

Rangel, Earl, 119, 120
Rapetti, Luca, 019
Raymond, William "Bill", 073
Rea, Brian F., 064, 072-073, 104
Red Onion Cocktail, 117
Redhead Cocktail, 117
Rednik Cocktail, 117
Reed, Claire L., 064, 099
Regan, Gary "Gaz", 008
Renzo's Dream Cocktail, 118
Rhonda's Dream Cocktail, 118
Repetty, Albert J., 064, 076, 093, 097, 098, 099, 102, 115, 128
Rettino, John A., 044, 064, 087, 090, 091, 118, 119, 125
Revere House Restaurant, 070
Road Runner Cocktail, 118
Roasted Russian Cocktail, 118
Roberta Cocktail, 118
Roberts, Marsha, 070
Robin Cocktail, 118
Robinson, Harold E., 127
Rodriquez, Armando, 095, 117
Rodriguez, Emilio, 064
Rodriguez, Rafael, 117
Rose Blossom Cocktail, 119
Rose Royce Cocktail, 119
Rovner, Sam, 065
Ruiseco, Jose, 028, 065, 076, 081, 105, 122, 129
Rum Passion Cocktail, 119
Rum Runner Cocktail, 076, 119
Rum-Ba Cocktail, 119

Rusty Dusty Cocktail, 119
Rychly, James, 079

S

Sam's #1 Cocktail, 120
Sam's #2 Cocktail, 120
Sand Piper Cocktail, 120
Sandoval, Caesar, 071, 076, 086, 118, 123
Sansone, Richard, 065, 122
Santa Ana Elks Lodge, 068
Sapphire Cocktail, 120
Sardi's Restaurant, 061
Satin Doll Cocktail, 120
Satin Glow Cocktail, 120
Satin Sheets Cocktail, 121
Saturn Cocktail, 034-036, 77, 121
Saturn #2 Cocktail, 002, 077, 121
Save the Saturn Society, 036
Savoy Cocktail Book, 004
Savoy Hotel, 008
Scandia Restaurant, 019-020
Schmidt, John, 064
Scotch Frog Cocktail, 121
Scotch Kist Cocktail, 121
Scvhistory.com, 070
Secret Harbor Cocktail, 121
Seeber, Kevin, 008, 013
Sexy Marie Cocktail, 122
Sherwood, Jack T., 076, 119, 121
Silverman, Milt, 065
Silver Nut Cocktail, 122
Simpson, Walter, 026, 076, 105
Sisko, Alex, 115
Skipperette Cocktail, 122
Sky Ranch Foundation, 032
Skyliner Cocktail, 122
Slow Maggie Cocktail, 122
Smith, Carmen, 070
Smuggler's Cove, 036

Sonora Cocktail Cocktail, 122
Sonora Sneak Cocktail, 123
Spanish Flu, IX
Spanish Gold Cocktail, 123
Spanish Kiss Cocktail, 123
Speakeasy, 002
Spear, Alan D., 109
Special 69 Cocktail, 123
Special Lady Cocktail, 123
Sperdakos, George, 064, 085, 119, 125
Spider's Web Cocktail, 014-015, 123
Stambaugh, Patrick J., 078
Star of Earth Cocktail, 036
Steller, M, 044
Stenger, Tom, 065, 072, 076, 108
Stern's Famous BBQ, 014, 019
Stiletto Cocktail, 124
Stink Okole Cocktail, 124
Stocker, David, 094, 097
Stokes, David, 024
Strawberry Blond Cocktail, 124
Sullivan, Robert, 107
Sun-kissed Margarita, 024
Sun Kiss Cocktail, 124
Sun Life Cocktail, 124
Sundor Cocktail, 124
Supnet, Benny, 064
Supnet, Rick, 065, 090
Surf & Sand Hotel, 034
Swanson, Carl, 086, 094, 122
Swanson, Ray, 044, 101
Sweet-Peach Cocktail, 125
Swinney, Al, 064
Swiss Barkeeper Union, 002
Sword, David L., 089
Sylvia's Dream Cocktail, 125

T

Takahashi, Ricky, 065

Takasaki, Earl, 065, 086, 116
Tam O'Shanter (tavern), 017
Tamashiro, Brian, 064
Tarling, William "Bill", 004, 006, 083
Tea By George Cocktail, 125
Tempo Cocktail, 125
Tequaize Cocktail, 125
The Deans of Drinks, 007
The Islands Bar, 034
Think Campero Cocktail, 125
Thomas, Jerry, 007
Tiki, 013, 034
Tinker Bell Cocktail, 126
Tio Popo Cocktail, 126
Tip's Jardine, 061 – 062
Tipsy Cocktail, 126
T'K.O. II Cocktail, 126
Tommy's Margarita, 023, 126
Toon, Norman, 065, 126
Toot Cocktail, 126
Tootsie Cocktail, 127
Top Banana Cocktail, 127
Top of Waikiki Restaurant, 050
Topaze Cocktail, 127
Trinidad Cocktail, 127
Tropea, Virgil, 089, 102, 109
Tuacian Cocktail, 127
Tulsaworld.com, 031
Tropical Itch Cocktail, 050

U

UKBG-USA East Coast Bartenders' Guild, 019, 073
UKBG-USA West Coast Bartenders' Guild, 018-020, 031, 034
Underwood, Vern, 022
United Kingdom Bartenders' Guild (UKBG), 02, 04, 07, 014, 017, 031
Universal Cocktail, 127

Universe Cocktail, 061, 128
Urban Transit Cocktail, 066
USBA, 052, 056
USBG Cocktail, 038-040, 128
USBG Florida chapter, 055
USBG Hawaii chapter, 055
USBG Illinois chapter, 055
USBG Las Vegas Chapter, VIII
USBG Puerto Rico Chapter, 055
USBG San Francisco Chapter, 023
USBG Master Accreditation Program, VI

V

Valentine's Charity Dinner-Dance, 032
Valley Orchard Cocktail, 128
Van Hagen, John, 001–002
Vance, Edward, 123
Vasquez, Armando, 064
Velvet Kiss Cocktail, 128
Villar, Angel, 123
Voderic Cocktail, 128
Vodka Gimlet Supreme Cocktail, 128
Volcanic Rumble Cocktail, 129

W

Warlina Cocktail, 129
Waterproof Cocktail, 129
Watson, Robert "Bob", 065, 079
Wayman, Gay, 065, 070
Weall, Robert H., 065, 088, 118
Wei, Richard, 036
Weidman, William, 112
Wescott, Wells, 079, 098
Whiskey Smash Cocktail, 129
White Lady Cocktail, 008
Whitfield, B., 006-007
Wikipedia, 001
Willard, Jack, 129
Williams, Everett, 116

Wine, Spirit, and Catering Trades Exhibition, 007
Winner's Cup Cocktail, 129
Wirstuk, Hank, 047, 085, 095
Wondrich, David, 023, 031
Wood, Noreen, 065
World Cocktail Competition (WCC), 049
World War I, IX, 001
World War II, IX, 001, 019

X

X-15 Cocktail, 034

Y

Yatco, Jose C., 047, 076, 096
Ycoy, Al, 083, 113, 116
Yee, Harry, 050
Yoon, Song Jun, 080
Young's Market, 017

Z

Zamuto, Peter, 044, 065, 076, 094, 127
Zangari, Tony, 065
Zinger Cocktail, 071, 129
Zombie Cocktail, 019